Exploring Cultural Communication
From the Inside Out

══ AN ETHNOGRAPHIC TOOLKIT ══

Exploring Cultural Communication
From the Inside Out

== AN ETHNOGRAPHIC TOOLKIT ==

Tabitha Hart

San José State University

Bassim Hamadeh, CEO and Publisher
Todd R. Armstrong, Publisher
Tony Paese, Project Editor
Alia Bales, Production Editor
Abbie Goveia, Senior Graphic Designer
Trey Soto, Licensing Coordinator
Natalie Piccotti, Director of Marketing
Kassie Graves, Senior Vice President of Editorial
Jamie Giganti, Director of Academic Publishing

Cover image copyright © 2015 Depositphotos/tai11.

Printed in the United States of America.

3970 Sorrento Valley Blvd., Ste. 500, San Diego, CA 92121

BRIEF CONTENTS

DETAILED CONTENTS

Chapter 4   Metacommunication   49

Chapter 5   Cognitive Scripts   71

Chapter 6   Norms, Rules, and Premises   85

Chapter 7   Speech Events   109

Chapter 8   Speech Codes   125

PREFACE

What do you do when you are a newcomer in a cultural group and you must find your way? From the perspective of an ethnographer of communication, one of the most effective strategies you can take is to go from the inside out. Start by immersing yourself in your new environment. Be observant as you participate in daily life, watch what happens, ask questions, document what you see and hear. Most importantly, pay very close attention to people's communication to inductively learn vital information about the local culture.

This workbook offers a hands-on crash course in exactly this process, making the tools used by ethnographers of communication accessible to all readers.

This book was born out of my own experience, education, and training in the art of navigating cultures. In between stints of graduate school, I spent roughly 7 years teaching English as a foreign language (EFL) in places where I was an absolute newcomer, including Japan, the Czech Republic, and Germany. Like my students, I was a foreign language learner attempting to master the mechanics of the languages spoken around me. However, my language teaching and language learning experiences illustrated that simply using the right words or applying the correct grammar wasn't enough. Without understanding the local unspoken expectations and rules undergirding communication, competency wasn't possible. This experience inspired me to pursue first an MA and then a PhD in communication studies, focusing specifically on intercultural and cultural communication. Along the way I was mentored by a renowned ethnographer of communication who taught me that, with the right tools in hand, any of us can use rigorous, interpretive fieldwork to study communication and understand the different cultures, broadly defined, that we find ourselves part of. The mission of this book is to put those tools into readers' hands.

By learning to apply the ethnography of communication approach to navigating (new) cultural environments, readers of this book will develop richer and more nuanced understandings not only of the different cultures that they are members of but also their own roles in an increasingly multicultural and global society.

Features and Benefits

This book is distinctive in the following six ways.

First, this book is unique in that it focuses on the interpretive theoretical/methodological framework of the **ethnography of communication (EC)** and **speech codes theory (SCT)**. The EC/SCT approach provides readers with an empirically proven way to understand local cultures from the inside out. This book will guide readers through the process of applying the EC/SCT approach to *any settings of their choice*. As far as I know, there is no other book on the market that does this.

Second, because the EC/SCT framework is useful for any type of cultural sojourner, *this book is written for a very broad audience*. Whether readers have just entered college; gotten a new job or joined a new company; moved to a different neighborhood, city, state, or country; or have even become part of a new team, club, organization, family, circle of friends, or any other type of group, whether physical or virtual, online or offline, this book is for them. We all go through the experience of having to find our feet in a new cultural environment, regardless of our age, background, or discipline, and this book provides a toolkit that can help anyone in that situation.

This book will be especially appealing for classes dealing with language and culture, including international and intercultural communication, linguistics and sociolinguistics, EFL and other foreign language learning, and study abroad courses. This is also a good book for courses covering communication theory, especially interpretive and/or intercultural theory; or methods, especially ethnography and action research. Additionally, this book is a good match for courses that focus on getting students involved in research and/or that foster citizen science.

Third, this book uses an *active learning approach* to support students as they *learn by doing*. When theoretical concepts are introduced, they are always paired with applied activities that require students to engage in fieldwork, data collection, and analysis. The culminating step of each chapter, and of the book, is learning how to make applied moves. Depending on the instructor's preferences, this book allows for the implementation of various *high-impact educational practices*, including producing, reviewing, and revising pieces of writing; participating in collaborative learning; engaging in research; and investigating different cultures and worldviews (Kuh, 2008).

Fourth, this book prioritizes *relevancy in its examples and applications*. While I have drawn on research exemplars dating from the 1960s all the way to the present day, I have done so strategically in order to emphasize topics and questions that remain highly salient to our students' lives and that, for better or for worse, are still pressing concerns today. Similarly, readers of this book are encouraged to use the EC/SCT approach to study aspects of their own lives and memberships within different cultural groups that they are currently contending with.

Fifth, this book treats **ethics** not as a one-time consideration but as something relevant at all stages of a research project. Ethical questions and issues are addressed in each chapter, emphasizing their importance throughout the research process.

Sixth, *this book can be used in traditional in-person courses as well as those taught in hybrid and remote/online modes.* In the section below I'll share some suggestions for using this book in any of these modes.

Organization and Suggestions for Use

Within each of the eight chapters there is a consistent and progressive sequence of activities. First, each chapter introduces students to the focal concept, how it has been studied by EC/SCT scholars, and why it is important. Next, students are introduced to practical, methodological, and ethical aspects of doing EC/SCT work. Then, the chapter guides students through a fieldwork activity. Students write a research memo to document and communicate what they observed and learned. Finally, they reflect on their experience and takeaways before moving on to the next chapter. An optional "deep dive" can be used to explore the concepts further.

This progressive approach is mirrored in the overarching structure of the book, which covers concepts, **units of analysis**, methods, and ethical issues in stages. For example, in Chapter 1 students select a field site; then, each subsequent chapter covers a different EC/SCT research focus and unit of analysis, going from small to large:

- Chapter 2: Speech Acts
- Chapter 3: Symbolic Terms
- Chapter 4: Metacommunication
- Chapter 5: Cognitive Scripts
- Chapter 6: Norms, Rules, and Premises
- Chapter 7: Speech Events
- Chapter 8: Speech Codes

The methods also progress in their scope and complexity from chapter to chapter. Students are introduced to immersive fieldwork right away, but there is a staged approach to what they are required to do while in the field:

- Chapter 2: Doing Observations and Creating Jottings in the Field
- Chapter 3: Collecting Textual Artifacts
- Chapter 4: Conducting Interviews
- Chapter 5: Doing Observations and Creating Recordings in the Field
- Chapter 6: Doing Observations and Writing Field Notes
- Chapter 7: Doing Observations and Combining Any of the Previous Methods
- Chapter 8: Working With a Whole Data Set

Likewise, the ethical issues are introduced in stages and are closely tied to the accompanying chapter material:

- Chapter 2: Revealing Your Research Intentions in the Field
- Chapter 3: Public Versus Private Data
- Chapter 4: Informed Consent
- Chapter 5: Anonymity
- Chapter 6: Vulnerability
- Chapter 7: Confidentiality
- Chapter 8: What to Do With Research Findings

Because of this, I suggest that students *work through the book in sequential order.*

Each chapter presents an opportunity to engage in fieldwork, data collection, data analysis, and reflections. In effect, the usual high-stakes final project is replaced with a short series of smaller, lower stakes projects, giving the students more opportunity not just to learn but also to revise and improve their work. Because of this, I suggest that students *submit, discuss, and evaluate chapter assignments regularly in order to provide formative assessment.*

As you facilitate your course, I recommend that you *combine collaborative and independent work as appropriate to your course.* Students in your class can select their own separate field sites, or they can use the same one(s). They can do their immersive fieldwork alone or in pairs or groups, as desired. There are advantages to all of these configurations, so choose the one that suits your class best.

For those who are *teaching online/remotely* (as I am at the time of this writing), *all of the activities in this book can be modified to suit your instructional mode.* When it comes to choosing a community to study and a specific field site to analyze, encourage your students to immerse themselves in a setting that is easily accessible to them, whether it is in person, online, or hybrid. For the in-class activities, you can run them synchronously in online class meetings (which is what I do via Zoom) or asynchronously as online discussions via your learning management system, whether Canvas or something else. Alternatively, these activities could be handled as free writes, journal entries, or even video responses.

Because of its workbook format, this book is designed to be written all over and is priced accordingly. Depending on whether they are using a hard or e-copy, *students can either write directly into this book or write/type out their assignments separately.* If the former, I recommend scanning and submitting work electronically. Free document scanning apps are useful for this purpose.

Acknowledgments

This book is a product of many years of education, training, mentorship, and collaboration within the ethnography of communication family. To all my fellow EC researchers and practitioners, thank you for the knowledge and the inspiration that your work provides. In particular, I extend special gratitude to the four scholars who generously reviewed my manuscript draft and whose feedback, suggestions, and encouragement truly helped me make this a better book:

Dr. Bradford "J" Hall, Utah State University
Dr. Evelyn Y. Ho, University of San Francisco
Dr. Gerry Philipsen, University of Washington
Dr. Michelle Scollo, College of Mount Saint Vincent

The idea for this book germinated while I was participating in the AANAPISI grant program at San José State University. I am grateful for the professional development and the release time that this opportunity provided, as well as the kind support of the program coordinators, Dr. Linda C. Mitchell, Michelle Hager, and Ann Baldwin.

Thank you to all of my students, from whom I continue to learn so much, including Irma Campos, who allowed excerpts from her COMM 154I jottings and field notes to be included in this book.

Thank you to my friend and colleague, Dr. Deanna Fassett, for giving me the gentle push that I needed to get this project off the ground.

Finally, my sincere thanks to the entire Cognella team, especially Todd Armstrong and Tony Paese at Cognella, whose assistance throughout this project, especially in the midst of the global COVID-19 pandemic and the CZU Lightning Complex Fires, helped me across the finish line.

I dedicate this labor to my dear friends and extended family, especially Hannes, Lucinda, Barry, Ralph, Jenna, Richard, and Vince, with all my love.

Navigating Cultures From the Inside Out

At the end of the 1990s, I moved to Berlin, Germany, on a whim. I had a bachelor's degree in communication studies and had taught English as a foreign language (EFL) for a few years in Japan and the Czech Republic. Most pertinently, although I spoke very little German, I had nonetheless managed to fall in love with a particular resident of that city, and so I was determined to settle in for a while.

Berlin at that time was still scarred—both literally and figuratively—by its past. To walk across the city was to stumble across memories of the ill-fated Weimar Republic, two World Wars, the Holocaust, the Cold War, and the country's miraculous reunification. With its ghosts still intact, the city of Berlin was slowly reclaiming its full status as the nation's capital city. Construction cranes filled the skyline. The cultural scene brought people from all over the world flocking in. Creative ventures abounded, businesses of all sorts were opening left and right, and the promises of possibility and reinvention were ripe.

Starbucks, the international coffee chain, was just one of the many prominent newcomers and quickly opened seven cafés in the most central districts of Berlin. As a college student in California, I had cut my teeth on Starbucks coffee, so I found this taste of home appealing. Practically from the moment of their grand opening, I became a regular patron, enthusiastically dropping in for a daily dose of caffeine. From my first visit onward, though, the Berlin Starbucks experience felt strangely off, despite the fact that so much of it replicated exactly what I was accustomed to from back home. At all the Berlin Starbucks cafés, things like the design and layout, background music, free bathroom access, uniforms, merchandise, and many menu items were familiar. So, too, was the customer service style, except that it was performed in German instead of English—and *that* was precisely what struck such an odd note. The Berlin baristas were making eye contact with customers, smiling at them, engaging them in small talk, and asking them for their names. While none of these things would have caused me to bat an eye back home, they all felt extremely unnatural in Berlin.

The reason for my confused response to the Starbucks customer service was that it went so starkly against the infamous Berliner *Schnauze*. The literal meaning of the word *Schnauze* is "snout," but its connotative meaning is "brashness" or "sassiness," which

Berliners are renowned for. For example, a customer in a Berlin restaurant might ask the server, *"Kann ich zahlen, bitte?"* ("Can I pay, please?") and get this snappy retort: *"Ich weiss nicht ob sie können, aber sie müssen!"* ("I don't know if you can, but you must!"). Inside the Berlin Starbucks cafés, however, it was another world altogether. The baristas greeted customers with direct eye contact, friendly smiles, and a singsong *"Hallo! Was kann ich für dich tun?"* ("Hello, what can I do for you?"). This incongruously cheery service contrasted so sharply with the usual Berlin gruffness that it threw me off.

Anthropologists have a name for moments like the one that I experienced at the Berlin Starbucks café: **rich points**. Rich points are those instances when a person feels sudden "incomprehensible surprise" and "unmet expectation" at what is going on in their immediate environment (Agar, 1999, 2006a, 2006b; Sandel, 2015). Oftentimes, experiencing a rich point suggests that you are brushing up against a "boundary" between different cultures (Agar, 1999, 2006a, 2006b).

An important point to emphasize here is that international travel is not a requirement for experiencing rich points or engaging in intercultural communication. Even if we never travel farther than our own neighborhoods, all of us will still be cultural sojourners at different moments in our lives. We will find ourselves as "newcomers" when we leave high school for college; start a new job or join a new company; move to a different neighborhood, city, or state; or become part of a new team, club, organization, family, circle of friends, or any other type of group, whether physical or virtual, online or offline.

Now it's your turn to think of a rich point that you have had. Reflect on a moment when you were a newcomer trying to find your feet in a new environment. What was an instance when you felt "incomprehensible surprise" or "unmet expectation," one in which you observed people being, acting, and/or relating in ways that were different to what you were accustomed to? What happened, and how did you respond? Jot down the particulars of your experience below.

Were you ever able to decode the rich point that you described? If so, how? What did you learn about the meaning or significance of that moment? What was the explanation or reason for it? If you were not able to decode the rich point, why not?

When I had my puzzling experience at the Berlin Starbucks cafés, it ignited my curiosity. I wondered why the Berlin baristas were performing customer service in this overtly friendly manner and how they felt about it. I questioned how customers perceived it, too, most of whom probably walked into Starbucks expecting the local *Schnauze*, just like me. Were they as startled by the American-styled service as I was? Did they take satisfaction in it, or did it leave them discomfited? At the time, I didn't know how to answer these questions, and it wouldn't be until years later when I pursued an MA and then a PhD in communication studies that I began learning intercultural communication theories and methodologies in earnest. In particular, I received rigorous training in a scientifically grounded, theoretical/methodological approach for navigating cultures called the ethnography of communication. I even ended up doing my own research on the customer service communication at the Berlin Starbucks cafés. (I also married that Berliner ☺.) This book is a culmination of all my cultural sojourning and education thereon. Recognizing that we all have to navigate new cultural terrain at various points in our lives (K. L. Fitch, 2005; Leeds-Hurwitz, 2005; Philipsen, 2010b), I hope that this book will offer you a map for finding your way.

Understanding Culture From the Inside Out

As social scientists, communication studies scholars typically pair theories and methods to investigate and answer research questions about their topics of interest. For intercultural communication scholars, there are a vast number of theories and methods to choose from. This book covers one specific framework: the ethnography of communication (Hymes, 1962, 1972a, 1977) and speech codes theory (Philipsen, 1992, 1997; Philipsen et al., 2005). Used together, the **ethnography of communication (EC)** and **speech codes theory (SCT)** can help you carefully, methodically, and systematically study a culture from the inside out, using your own powers of observation to see, hear, document, and analyze how people communicate and what that communication means to them (Philipsen, 2010a).

The ethnography of communication (Hymes, 1962, 1972a, 1977) was born out of and is closely related to traditional ethnography. Ethnography is a research-based approach to understanding the social world; to use it, researchers immerse themselves in cultural settings where, through sustained participant observation, they attempt to understand those settings from the perspectives of the locals (Wolcott, 1999).

EC/SCT scholars use ethnography to study **communication** (Philipsen, 1990), a catch-all term for any type of social interaction, from face-to-face and verbal speech to nonverbal, text-based, technology-mediated communication and more (Carbaugh, 2005). By doing this, EC scholars aim to make discoveries about local cultures (Keating, 2001). SCT scholars then take their research to the next level by using speech codes theory (Philipsen, 1992, 1997; Philipsen et al., 2005) to develop explanations and predictions about culture and communication. This gives them the potential to offer strategic advice and insight that can help people make better choices in their cultural environments (Sprain & Boromisza-Habashi, 2013).

In short, the EC/SCT framework can help you better understand and navigate a cultural locale such that you can more effectively devise communication strategies and (ideally) achieve your desired goals. This book will teach you the ins and outs of using the EC/SCT approach toward studying a local culture from the inside out.

Culture From an EC/SCT Perspective

Before getting further into *how* EC/SCT scholars research culture and cultural communication, let's first look at *what* they consider culture to be. From an EC/SCT perspective, culture and communication are inextricably linked together. In fact, EC/SCT scholars don't equate culture with "a place, country, or group" (Philipsen, 2010b, p. 162); instead, they essentially see culture as communication (Philipsen, 1987,

1992, 2003). More precisely, SCT defines culture as a **speech code**; that is, a set of beliefs about communicative conduct, including (but not limited to) the symbols, norms, rules, premises, and values that people use to guide their communication (Philipsen, 1987, 1997). People use speech codes to understand the world around them and to evaluate it, organize it, operate within it, and even challenge it (Carbaugh, 1995, 2005, 2015; Philipsen, 1987, 1990, 1992, 2003). From this, we can infer that EC/SCT scholars are interested in examining the following aspects of communication:

- Communicative symbols and their meanings
- Premises and rules about communicative conduct; that is, the underlying assumptions and guidelines that people have about communication and how to engage in it
- Meanings related to communicative conduct; that is, what certain communicative acts mean to people and why
- People's beliefs and values about communication
- How and why people use communication to get things done in the world and what this reveals about their belief systems

Each chapter of this book will walk you through the process of identifying a particular aspect of communication to examine using the EC/SCT approach. You will also learn how to examine and draw links between communication and the local culture that it is part of.

Methods for EC/SCT Data Collection and Analysis

With the EC/SCT approach, the discovery process is not random or haphazard but structured and methodical (Philipsen, 1990). EC/SCT researchers learn how to search for and scrutinize specific aspects of cultural communication and also how to utilize best practices for social scientific and ethnographic work.

Consistent with its ethnographic roots, the EC/SCT approach requires that we study communication from the perspectives of the people who are engaging in and experiencing it, exploring what it means to them on their own terms, in the context of their social worlds (Lindlof & Taylor, 2011; Philipsen, 1992; Tracy, 2013). In practical terms, most EC/SCT scholars collect data in real-life settings (rather than laboratory or experimental ones) where they can see and hear people's actual, day-to-day communication (Hymes, 1964, 1972a; Philipsen, 2010b; Philipsen & Coutu, 2005). Doing this often requires EC/SCT researchers to spend time engaging in immersive fieldwork at designated field sites, where they do observations or participant observations on the communication taking place there (Keating, 2001; Philipsen, 1990, 2010b; Saville-Troike, 2003). As part of their fieldwork, EC/SCT researchers spend time with their research participants, carefully observing and interacting with them, and often interviewing them as well (Philipsen, 1990, 2010b). To be as systematic and as rigorous as possible (Carbaugh, 1995, 2007a), they often collect large amounts of data, including jottings and field notes, images and recordings, interviews, and other texts and artifacts.

Once they have collected their data, EC/SCT researchers use **qualitative data analysis** methods to look for emergent patterns (Hymes, 1962; Lindlof & Taylor, 2011; Philipsen, 1992; Saville-Troike, 2003; Tracy, 2013), sometimes focusing on reoccurring phenomena and other times examining unusual or anomalous moments. To determine if what they are learning is true and accurate, EC/SCT scholars do **member checks** (Lindlof & Taylor, 2011; Tracy, 2013), soliciting feedback from the people whom they are studying. For example, they may present their emergent findings to community members and ask them if their findings are correct (Saville-Troike, 2003).

Each chapter of this book will help you learn how to use EC/SCT to watch, listen, analyze, and understand communication in different cultural communities. You'll try out methods of data collection like observations, interviews, and gathering textual artifacts. You'll learn how to process and analyze the **data** that you collect and how to extrapolate research **findings**.

Developing an EC/SCT Frame of Mind

According to the EC/SCT perspective, we must all inevitably come to terms with different cultures in our lives, whether or not we ever fully join them (Philipsen, 1990, 2010b). In contending with different cultures, there is always the potential for confusion, misalignment, mistakes, or even conflict (Boromisza-Habashi, 2017). The EC/SCT framework is a useful tool not just for decoding a culture but also for diagnosing and addressing clashing codes when they occur (Coutu, 2000, 2008; Huspek, 1994). Because of this, EC/SCT scholars—like many other social scientists—may find themselves running toward conflict rather than away from it as part of their research process.

This behooves EC/SCT scholars to be critically reflective about their own motives, processes, and judgments as they engage in their research. They must be prepared to unpack their own values, which implicitly shape every aspect of their work, from the research questions that they pose to their choice of communities to work with, their immersion in field sites, their emphasis on privileging participants' voices, and so on.

Then there is the question of what to do with their research findings. Many EC/SCT scholars share an ethic of suspending judgment and not evaluating or attempting to change people's realities while studying them (Carbaugh, 1989–1990; Philipsen, 1989–1990, 2010b). Historically, though, an aim of EC research has been to foster greater understanding, enhance empathy, productively resolve conflict, and promote a more just society (Blommaert, 2009; Saville-Troike, 2003).

This book will help you develop an EC/SCT researcher's frame of mind, including how to be more cognizant of your own subjectivities in the research process.

Engaging Ethically

All researchers, regardless of their philosophies, theories, or methods, are responsible for acting **ethically**—that is, in a morally correct manner—as they conduct their research, from beginning to end. Just like other researchers, EC/SCT scholars must grapple with how to be ethical, answering questions like the following:

- How do we determine what is worth researching or knowing about, and what are the implications for that?
- (When) do you tell people that you are studying them, and what exactly do you say?
- How do you ask for people's permission to study them?
- When, if ever, are you allowed to record people's communication?
- To what extent should we be involved in a community in which we are also doing research?
- What should we do with the things that we learn? Are we allowed to use our findings to promote social change?

This book will help you articulate and engage with important ethical questions that arise when doing EC/SCT research.

Learning by Doing

The EC/SCT framework is a highly practical, fieldwork-based framework for finding your feet in a new cultural environment. As Gerry Philipsen (1992), the originator of speech codes theory, wrote:

> An ethnographer of [communication] is a naturalist, who watches, listens, and records communicative conduct in its natural setting. The ethnographer describes what is to be found in a given speech community as well as what regular patterns can be observed there. (p. 7)

Accordingly, this book takes a hands-on approach toward learning EC/SCT. This means that, by using this book, you'll engage in a lot of learning by doing. Each chapter poses a series of activities on the interpretive processes of engaging in, observing, analyzing, and understanding a cultural environment from the inside out.

Using this book, you will gain hands-on experience in doing ethnographic research. You'll develop skills for choosing and entering a field site, engaging with people at your site, collecting and analyzing data, developing evidence-based claims, verifying your findings, and navigating ethical issues.

Choosing a Community and a Field Site

As you work through this book, you'll be conducting your own fieldwork on a community of your choosing. For our purposes, we are defining **community** as a group of people who share a feeling of commonality with one another, whether that feeling is based on their common interests, identities, affiliations, professions, roles, jobs, language(s), traditions, responsibilities, goals, or any other factor (Milburn, 2004, 2015b; Philipsen, 1987). With this open and flexible definition, your community of interest could be online, offline, or hybrid; large or small; and nascent or well-established.

Ideally, the community that you study should also be one that you are connected to and want to understand better. Therefore, take a moment now to reflect on the different communities that you have been or are currently a member of. List some of those communities below.

-
-
-
-
-

Looking at your list, which of the communities that you identified are you still in the process of trying to navigate? Which ones would you like to understand better? In which ones have you experienced a rich point, or something that surprised, perplexed, or confused you? Jot down your thoughts below.

_____

_____

_____

_____

_____

_____

_____

_____

Now, look back at your list again, but this time consider the following practicalities:

- Which of the communities do you currently have connections to? What is the nature of your connections? If you don't have connections (how) would you be able to establish some in order to do the fieldwork that this book requires?

- Which of the communities would you be able to regularly access while using this book?

- Do you need any special knowledge, skills, or tools to access or to function within any of the communities on your list?

- How well do you speak the language(s) of the communities that you identified?

Jot down your responses below.

_____

_____

_____

_____

_____

_____

_____

_____

_____

_____

_____

The moment of choosing and committing to a community to do ethnographic research on is a weighty one. Set yourself up for success by choosing one that you are both interested in and that you can realistically access for the duration of your project.

Now, with this in mind, which community do you think you'd like to choose to focus on, and why? What is it about this community that piques your interest? What do you hope to learn about it? In what ways would learning more about this community benefit you?

Finally, having selected a community to study, what associated field site(s) could you see yourself spending time in for your fieldwork, and why? Briefly describe them below and include a few sentences about your rationale for selecting them. How will you access these sites? What possible challenges, obstacles, or considerations do you anticipate needing to work through as you do so?

_____

_____

_____

_____

_____

_____

_____

_____

The remaining chapters of this book will guide you through the process of using the EC/SCT approach to scientifically explore and understand the community that you have chosen. Now it's time to get started!

Optional Deep Dive

▶ For more information on choosing a field site, visit the University of Southern California Center for Religion and Civic Culture report titled "How Do You Choose and Gain Access to a Field Site?" at https://tinyurl.com/y5ag74om.

▶ Another site to explore is the online Field Research Methods Lab hosted by the London School of Economics Saw Swee Hock Southeast Asia Centre at https://tinyurl.com/y54nd48v.

Speech Acts

Definition of Speech Acts

The academic year has begun at your new university, and you have arrived at your very first class. It is scheduled to begin in a few minutes, and students are trickling in. You take a seat in the middle of the room and look around. The professor is standing at a podium, staring intently at their computer. Scattered around the quiet room are 20 or so other students, most of whom are busy with their cell phones. It's very warm and bound to get even warmer as the sun shines in through the large, closed windows, which line one entire wall. As you begin to perspire, you find yourself wishing for a cool breeze. What should you do? In other circumstances you might simply move over to the bank of windows and open one. Here, however, you are new and aren't sure what the protocol is. Because of this, you decide to check in with the other people in the room and make a request to open a window.

Making a request is one type of **speech act**, a communicative activity that has a "specified pragmatic intent" (Saville-Troike, 2003, p. 161; Searle, 1969); that is, a particular, practical function. Put differently, every speech act serves a specific purpose. For example, the purpose of making a request is to voice a wish and hopefully get others to comply with it. The very name of this concept, *speech act*, emphasizes the performative nature of communication and how it is enacted or done to accomplish things in the world. The concept of a speech act also points to how we intentionally and strategically use communication to achieve our desired results.

There are, of course, many more types of speech acts besides making requests, some of which are listed in Table 2.1. Have a look at the list and circle the speech acts that you have engaged in recently. How would you describe the pragmatic intent—that is, the purpose—of each one? Try doing this as precisely as you can, following the first example. What additional speech acts can you think of? Jot them down at the end of the list.

TABLE 2.1 Speech Acts and Their Pragmatic Intent

Speech Act	Pragmatic Intent; that is, the Purpose of the Speech Act
Agreeing	*The pragmatic intent of agreeing is to express that you think or feel the same way as another person or to show that you consent to whatever it is they are proposing. It shows alignment with the thoughts, feelings, or actions of another person.*
Apologizing	
Complaining	
Complimenting	
Criticizing	
Demanding	
Denying	
Disagreeing	
Enthusing	
Flattering	
Instructing	
Joking	
Objecting	
Opining	

(continued)

TABLE 2.1 Speech Acts and their Pragamatic Intent   *(continued)*

Speech Act	Pragmatic Intent; that is, the Purpose of the Speech Act
Persuading	
Promising	
Refusing	
Suggesting	
Sympathizing	
Thanking	
Warning	
Write in any other speech acts that you can think of.	

Why Speech Acts Matter

For any given speech act, there are numerous ways to communicate it, whether orally; in writing; or nonverbally through gestures, pictures, or other symbolic forms. Despite the name, then, speech acts are actually best thought of as *communicative* activities, not just speaking ones. For example, you could point to a closed window and mime opening it. You could text your request to someone rather than uttering it aloud. You could use a single word like "open" with a questioning tone while making a meaningful glance at the windows. If you decided to fully vocalize your request, you could phrase it in many different ways, whether directly and casually, elaborately and formally, or anywhere in between. Table 2.2, for example, presents 10 different ways to phrase the request to have a window opened.

TABLE 2.2 Requests to Open a Window

1.	Hey, open that window for me, OK?
2.	Oh man, it's hot. Can you open a window or something?
3.	Could I get you to open that window?
4.	Would you mind opening that window?
5.	Sorry to bother you, but could you open a window?
6.	Excuse me, could you open that window, please?
7.	Is there any way you could open that window for me?
8.	Would you be so kind as to open that window?
9.	I'd be so grateful if you could open that window.
10.	If it's not too much trouble, could you possibly open that window?

Which of the phrasings from Table 2.2 would you feel inclined to use when making your request about the classroom window, and with whom (fellow students or the professor)? Why? Which of them would you avoid using, and why?

All of the phrases in Table 2.2 have the same pragmatic intent, or basic function, which is to make a request (in this case, to open a window), but they are different in their tone and style. The phrases at the top of the list are more direct and informal; their style is terse and unelaborated. Conversely, the phrases at the end of the list use more softening language, and some of them express more ingratiation with the addressee, potentially conferring additional respect. To what extent did this factor into your answers above?

Now look back at the list of speech acts in Table 2.1. Choose one and brainstorm different ways that you could phrase it, listing them below. Once your list is complete, reflect on what makes the phrases different from one another.

1.

2.

3.

4.

5.

6.

7.

8.

9.

10.

What is it that leads communicators to choose one way out of many possible ways to perform a speech act? The answer to this question relates to the reason speech acts are so important: namely, that all speech acts are performed in particular cultural contexts involving culturally significant elements, such as settings; participants and their relationships with one another; activities and goals; norms, premises, and rules, and so on. Each of these different elements shapes how people choose to engage in and respond to speech acts.

The **setting** or **scene** of the communicative activity is the location where it takes place. This could be a physical place like a classroom, beach, or city street, or it could be a geographical area like a city, state, region, or country. Settings can also be online or virtual, whether the immersive world of an MMORPG (massively multiplayer online role-playing game), a web-based community such as LinkedIn, or even an app like TikTok. Regardless of the type of place, the setting exerts a strong influence on how people perceive, engage in, and respond to speech acts.

Take, for example, the speech act of complimenting someone's appearance, which research demonstrates is a very common type of compliment (Ishihara, 2010). If you were sitting in the university classroom described at the beginning of this chapter, how would you feel about giving or receiving any of the following compliments?

- "Your haircut looks great."
- "I like your shirt, it really looks good on you."

- "Nice bag!"
- "Your makeup looks so professional."

In some contexts it might be acceptable, or even desirable, to be told that you look good; for example, if a friend complimented your appearance at work or school, that might be perfectly alright (Fong, 1998; Ishihara, 2010). However, imagine that you were on your own, walking down a public street. How would you feel about giving or receiving any one of the same compliments to or from a stranger walking by you? If, in the public street setting, you would feel uncomfortable, then your response is consistent with research indicating that giving compliments to unknown passersby on the street is generally viewed as inappropriate (Bailey, 2016, 2017a).

Related to this, of course, is the question of the *participants*; that is, who is involved in any given speech act, what identities they subscribe to (or have ascribed to them), and the nature of their relationships with one another. For example, language that is direct and casual—such as phrases 1 through 4 from Table 2.2—is likely to be used when addressing someone who is equal or lower in rank, or perhaps someone with whom the relationship is so close that no softening is required. More polite language—such as phrases 6 through 10 from Table 2.2—could suggest that the speakers don't know each other well or that the addressee is of higher status or rank (see K. Fitch & Sanders, 1994, for more on this). Similarly, in the example of giving personal compliments, while it may be fine to praise the appearance of someone close to you—like a significant other, a friend, a family member, and so on (Fong, 1998; Ishihara, 2010)—complimenting a stranger is often perceived as beyond the bounds of acceptability (Bailey, 2016, 2017a, 2017b); even more so with particular gender configurations, such as an unknown male complimenting the appearance of a female.

How people engage in and respond to speech acts is also shaped by the *type and nature of the communicative activity* going on at the scene. Let's go back to the speech act of making a request. If you were requesting something that, in your view, seemed very easy to fulfill, that would likely be reflected in how you formulated the request.

> *Could* you open the window?

> *Can* I borrow your pen for a minute?

> *May* I get by?

If, on the other hand, you were requesting something that seemed difficult or even downright onerous to fulfill, you would probably formulate your request differently.

> *Could you possibly* give me a ride home?

> *Would it be possible* for you to read this 30-page research paper and give me some feedback on it?

> *I hate to ask this, but is there any chance at all that you could* let me borrow a few thousand dollars?

In these examples, the more difficult the task is perceived to be, the more deferential the phrasing becomes. Such language can potentially demonstrate that the speaker knows that their request is a tough one. Alternatively, the more deferential phrasing could convey respect to the hearer, thereby softening the request and perhaps persuading them to acquiesce.

The desired **goals** that people have in mind also influence the ways in which they engage in speech acts. Implicit or "translucent" goals, on the other hand, are less obvious and may not even be directly articulated by the people involved in the speech act (K. Fitch & Sanders, 1994). For example, research on the speech act of joking and teasing within different communities reveals similar explicit goals but different translucent or implicit ones. As you might have guessed, the explicit goal of joking and teasing is generally to amuse people and provoke laughter. Within the Western Apache community, one implicit goal in making jokes about the behavior of the "Whiteman" was to engage in pointed social commentary about Anglo-American culture (Basso, 1979). Within groups of mushroom collectors and meteorologists, an implicit goal of joking was to dial down tension in moments of disagreement or conflict (Fine & De Soucey, 2005). Within a tight-knit circle of male friends, the implicit goal of teasing was to play down the differences in group members' identities and abilities (Robles, 2019). Across all of these different groups, other implicit goals of joking and teasing were to make members feel more connected and closer with one another and to reaffirm who was a member and who was not.

Unlike goals, the **outcomes** of speech acts may be unintentional. For example, research conducted on the speech act of advising suggests that when a person gives advice, they position themselves as knowing better, which can cause the recipient to feel put down (Goldsmith & Fitch, 1997). Therefore, a potential outcome of giving advice can sometimes be that the recipient feels resentment or offense, even when the advice giver has the best of intentions (Goldsmith & Fitch, 1997).

In every community, there are also local **norms**, **rules**, and **premises** that guide members' understandings of and expectations for speech acts. Chapter 6 of this book covers norms, rules, and premises in detail, but for now, let's briefly look at how they pertain to speech acts. Norms, rules, and premises influence people's beliefs about who should perform speech acts, under what circumstances, and how. For example, with the speech act of apologizing, one EC researcher found that, among Japanese speakers, there was an underlying norm that an apology carries responsibility for harm and therefore must demonstrate sufficient "concern for the other party who has been suffering" (Kotani, 2016, p. 138). The expectation for the Japanese speakers interviewed by this researcher was that the person who did something wrong ought to simply apologize for the suffering that they had caused and leave any explanations out of it. For example, if someone was late to an appointment and kept their friend waiting, they should just say something like "I'm so sorry I was late" and stop there. If the person who had caused offense included an explanation with their apology, as in "I'm so sorry I was late, traffic was really terrible," then it would actually cause even more offense because it would seem like an attempt to lessen their responsibility for what had happened, thereby weakening the apology.

The English speakers (primarily North Americans) that Kotani studied, on the other hand, felt that apologies were only warranted when a person was directly responsible for causing suffering. In these cases, offering an apology was a way of "admitting responsibility for causing the offence" (Kotani, 2002, p. 65). Furthermore, the English speakers thought it was perfectly appropriate to include explanations because doing so showed that, regardless of what happened, their intentions were positive. For example, if someone was late to an appointment and kept their friend waiting, they ought to begin by saying, "I'm so sorry I was late," and then follow up with more information, like "traffic was really bad," or "I tried calling you to let you know that I was going to be delayed." For the North American speakers, these sorts of explanations helped apologizers shift responsibility away from themselves, turning their actions "from offensive to unavoidable" (Kotani, 2016, p. 138).

Local norms, rules, and premises also shape how speech acts are performed, down to what kinds of language people use, in what order, with what tone, and so on. For example, a study on the unwritten rules guiding how to give and receive compliments suggests that in North American culture it is proper to accept them and to show appreciation for someone's praise. In this context, denying a compliment would appear rude and ungrateful. In Chinese culture, on the other hand, compliments should be politely denied as a way of showing modesty, while accepting a compliment would make the recipient appear overly proud and immodest (Fong, 1998).

To summarize, numerous contextual factors shape when, where, why, and how communicators perform speech acts. They also shape how speech acts are perceived, interpreted, evaluated, and responded to. When we go from one cultural context to another, it is reasonable to expect that speech acts will change, whether radically, slightly, or somewhere in between. In this way, speech acts are *cultural acts*, and this is precisely what makes studying them so valuable. Because speech acts are inextricably tied up with cultural contexts, studying them is effectively a means of analyzing and understanding culture.

Studying Speech Acts in the Field

If you have already spent some time at your field site, then draw on your memory to identify some of the common speech acts that you regularly engage in there or see others engaging in. Then write the speech acts below.

If you haven't yet spent time at your field site, now is a good time to start. For this activity, spend just 15 to 30 minutes at your site listening to and observing interactions between people. What speech acts can you identify? Write them down in the following box.

_____

_____

_____

_____

_____

_____

_____

_____

_____

_____

Reflect for a moment on the speech acts that you noted above. Are there any that seem really vital to your success within the community? Which ones seem especially important to your fellow group members? Which ones pique your curiosity? Choose one speech act that you would like to learn more about, and name it below.

The speech act that I will analyze in my community is ...

Ethics: Revealing Yourself and Your Research Intentions

In social scientific research, deception, defined as "any intentional choice by the researcher to create in participants a deliberate misperception pertaining to an essential element of the [research]" (Henningsen, 2018, p. 360), is used as a strategy to avoid influencing or biasing the data under study. Among ethnographers of communication, deception is generally avoided; instead, researchers opt for transparency and openness about what they are doing. The reason for this is that, as interpretive scholars, ethnographers of communication want to learn about people's lives, cultures, and experiences from _their_ perspectives, as openly and as accurately as possible; to do this, it is very helpful to have their acceptance and support (Creswell, 2013).

In keeping with this ethical code, you should be prepared to explain to people at your field site what kind of research you are doing and why. The key points that you should include in your explanation are as follows:

- Who you are and your role(s) at your field site
- Your topic(s) of interest; that is, what you are looking for/at
- The purpose of your data collection
- What you'll do with the data that you collect
- Your plan for protecting people's identities and what they share with you

In the space below, draft a short, written explanation that you could give about your observations to someone at your field site. For example:

> My name is Jane Doe, and I'm an intern here at Company XYZ. Right now I'm studying how people at this company make requests, including the kinds of phrases that they use. I'm doing this for a class project, and also, because I'm interested in the topic. I'm planning to type up my notes and use them to write a research paper for my class. I'll anonymize all of the material that I collect before I submit anything to my professor. I'm not going to share the information that I collect with anyone outside of my class.

Finally, if it happens that someone at your field site does not want to be observed, interviewed, and so on, then you should respect their wishes.

Fieldwork: Observations and Jottings

To study speech acts, you will need to closely observe how they play out in real-life interactions. In most cases it's likely that the speech acts that you are focusing on will simply occur, without advance notice or warning. For this reason, you'll need to be ready to capture your speech acts data on the fly. One way to do this is by creating jottings, which are rough notes that you quickly jot (i.e., write) down while you are observing or participating in communication activities at your field site; hence, their name (Emerson et al., 2011). **Jottings** are not a comprehensive account of your observations; rather, they are only simple notes, the purpose of which is to help you remember what you saw and heard. You can think of jottings as a kind of mental bookmark that helps you recall what you saw and experienced in the field. In this way they are similar to the notes that you might make while listening to a lecture or participating in a classroom workshop. Ethnographers use jottings as a basis for writing field notes, which are detailed descriptions of their observations. The process of transforming jottings into field notes will be covered in Chapter 6; for now, see Figure 2.1 for a nice example of jottings, written by Irma Campos, a student in one of my classes.

While you are observing and perhaps also participating in communication activities at your site, be on the lookout for occurrences of your chosen speech act. Then, when the speech act occurs, create your jottings then and there. It's fine to use very simple tools to do this, whether a plain paper notebook and a pen or even a cell phone app that you can type your jottings into. In any case, your jottings should include your own notes on the larger context (setting, participants, communication activity) as well as what people say and do (their words, gestures, etc.). At the very least, you should pay attention to the following:

- Where the speech act is taking place; that is, the scene or setting
- The main communication activities that are taking place in that moment, at that scene, out of which the speech act arises
- The people participating in the speech act, whether as speakers, listeners, or bystanders on the scene
- The words that people say and who says them
- What the goals of the speech act appear to be
- How the speech act plays out, including how people respond to it

Direct Observation	Interpretations
once I was finished stocking all the produce + eggs — Catherine told me to go to the register and read the "farmstand Trainng doc" — when it is/the opening and closing duties as well as how to properly make sales in the POS system in the iPad: The key things to remember	(I thought it was pretty well organized and stocked all materials)

everything was set and there was many extra bags and supplies in the drawers under the register |
| ▷ She explained that I had to weigh the oranges and everything else was sold by itself | |
| ▷ It took like 10 mins to set up and we got our first customer — she was very nice and talkative — she said that the produce "looked so yummy" | |

FIGURE 2.1 Jottings

Direct Observation	Interpretation
They have a sign in sheet for people who purchase produce	
— Continue small # is to use to re-apply for a grant.	
— the sign in sheet has: name, # of people zip code, phone number, email.	
→ As we were setting up people in the firm	
— gone to the entrance & youth survey directly across & began to need	
they worked together	the prices were less than at some grocery stores
— they worked slowly and steady	wonder how they can maintain the price to be low
they would look at me occasionally	
— we had more customers arrive may purchased carrots + lettuce	

FIGURE 2.1 *(continued)*

Direct observation	Interpretation(s)
I noticed that the customers were returning they already knew the process	One lady had a veggie voucher - it was worth $8. She knew exactly what to do, and the prices of the items
Many asked what types of vegetables were sold here and where they come from	I wonder how many times she has been here before?
Cashier had mentioned to me that some produce was from another farm	
Farm [illegible] ones, that [illegible] are collected from the homes of people in the neighboring community	
- She said ppl can sign up online to have their [illegible] harvested by the farm.	I think this is a perfect practice to utilize the food in the community and distribute it in a organized manner
The customers varied in demographics and were people who spoke [illegible] Spanish, [illegible] Creole.	

FIGURE 2.1 *(continued)*

If you are able to, follow the guidelines in Chapter 4 to interview people at the field site to learn more. For example, ask about the (unwritten) rules that people apply to the speech act, their feelings and opinions about the speech act, their goals and motivations for engaging in it, and how they feel about particular outcomes. If you know common cases of a particular occurrence of a speech act, you could also ask interviewees for their opinions about the specific interactions that you have observed, including whether it is considered successful, proper, appropriate, and so on.

Data Analysis

After you have created your jottings, use them as the basis for describing the speech acts that you observed in the field, following the format below. For now, describe just one instance of the speech act that you observed in as much detail as you can.

First, put the speech act down in writing as accurately as you can. When possible, include who said what to whom, and in what order. If you're unsure of some detail, write that down too—a common notation for this is (?).

Setting/Scene

Describe the setting/scene where the speech act occurred.

Communicative Activities

Describe the communicative activities that were going on at the scene when the speech act occurred.

Participants

Describe the participants who were on the scene when the speech act occurred. This should include people who were observing the speech act take place, as well as the people who were actually engaged in it.

Goals and Intentions

If possible, describe the participants' goals and intentions for the speech act, both explicit and implicit. Since you can't read the participants' minds, the best way to understand their goals and intentions is to look back at what they actually said and did and/or to directly ask them what their goals and intentions were. If you don't have this direct information, then you should note down that you are guessing or inferring people's goals and intentions.

Outcomes

Describe the outcomes of the speech act, as far as you can tell. In other words, what happened? How did people on the scene respond? What did they say and do? How did the speech act end?

Write a Research Memo

When ethnographers of communication study a speech act, they usually collect many instances of it so that they can look for patterns across interactions. If you only have a few interactions, or (in this case) just one, it will be difficult to see patterns and hard, if not impossible, to come up with generalizable findings. Nevertheless, you can still practice doing data analysis on the speech act that you observed, even if the amount of data is small.

In ethnographic and other qualitative research, a good way to do this is by writing up a research memo. **Research memos** are short, informally written accounts that the researcher creates at various stages in their project. During the data-collection phase but also especially when doing data analysis, writing research memos is an analytical move that will help you document, in writing, the interesting points and patterns that you are noticing in your data (Emerson et al., 2011; Lindlof & Taylor, 2019). For our purposes, research memos are especially helpful because they are preliminary rather than conclusive analyses of what you are seeing and learning about the communication and communities that you are studying.

For this research memo on speech acts, start by reflecting on the broad patterns that you noticed in the data that you collected. How would you explain the speech act that you studied? Describe the conditions under which it occurred; the specific words, phrases, gestures, and/or signs that people used to engage in the speech act; and the goals and outcomes of the speech act. Make sure that your memo is directly based on the data that you collected and described earlier in this chapter.

Check Your Work

Share your research memo with someone from your field site. Do they feel that it is accurate? Why or why not? Alternatively, share your findings with your classmates. Do you see any intriguing similarities or differences across one another's field sites?

_____

_____

_____

_____

_____

_____

_____

_____

_____

Reflections and Recommendations

Before moving on to the next chapter, take a moment to jot down some of your reflections, questions, ideas, and recommendations on the work that you just did, answering any of the following questions.

1. What were your main takeaways from doing this work?

2. Did you make any "bonus" discoveries that weren't necessarily related to the main concepts that you were studying? Ethnographers often end up with interesting data that isn't directly relevant to what they are focusing on. Rather than throwing those data away, make note of them here in case you'd like to follow up at a later time.

3. Did you have any difficulties or disappointing results when you did this work? If yes, don't worry; this is a natural part of doing ethnographic research and something that you can definitely learn from. Take a moment to reflect on any setbacks here. What were they, and why do you think they occurred? How might you avoid them if you were to do this work again?

4. What do's and don'ts would you pass on to your future self if you were to study the concepts covered in this chapter again? What would you do differently, and why?

5. What additional questions arose while you were doing this work? If you were going to continue with or expand this work, what would you want to explore? How might you deepen or expand your work?

6. What other placeholders, notes, or reminders would you like to set down for yourself here?

_____

Optional Deep Dive

► For more information on speech acts, visit the Center for Advanced Research on Language Acquisition (CARLA) website at https://tinyurl.com/yyw662ho

► CARLA's online resources include a searchable bibliography of speech act research, including studies on specific speech acts like cursing, disagreeing, promising, and so on. https://tinyurl.com/y29zqkdw

► The Center for Open Educational Resources and Language Learning (COERLL) at the University of Texas at Austin has a series of online tutorials on foreign language teaching methods. The one on pragmatics includes a brief overview of speech acts as well as some interesting examples: https://tinyurl.com/y2ancmqp

Symbolic Terms

Definition of Symbolic Terms

Imagine that you are texting a friend about your shared plans for Friday night. "How about if you pick me up from work at 7:30, and then we have dinner before meeting everybody else?" you write. A few moments later you get a reply from your friend; it doesn't contain any words, only a single emoji depicting a hand clenched in a fist, with the thumb sticking straight up. How would you interpret your friend's response?

For many people around the world, the thumbs-up is a symbol of approval or agreement. A **symbol** is something—a sign, mark, gesture, action, image, person, and so on—that represents or stands in for something else. In the case of the text message described

FIGURE 3.1 *Thumbs-up symbol*

above, the thumbs-up emoji *symbolizes* something akin to "Yes, sounds good," "I agree," or "Sure." Symbols are a powerful form of communication because of their potential to communicate complex ideas, values, and meanings simply and quickly. Put differently, a symbol is a kind of shorthand language that is instantly intelligible to members of a cultural group who share the same understanding of its meaning.

In addition to gestures and pictures, all letters, characters, and words can be considered symbols because they convey or express ideas, values, and meanings. Accordingly, we can accurately say that symbols are ever present in our cultural worlds, appearing everywhere any type of communication occurs, whether written, verbal, or nonverbal.

As a member of various cultural groups, you are already an adept symbol user. Just by living, working, and playing in a community, you have developed your own literacy in that group's symbols. In fact, you probably know how to read thousands of your group's symbols.

What, for example, do the following things symbolize to you? Write your answers down next to the symbols.

Symbol	Symbolic Meaning
A red rose	
Clenching your fist, bending your elbow so that your upper arm is parallel to your body, then drawing your forearm down in a quick pumping motion	
An area of painted white stripes going across a road	

If your interpretation of these symbols is based on a North American cultural sensibility, then your answers were probably the following: that a red rose symbolizes romantic love and passion, the clenched fist gesture is a sign of victory or triumph, and an area of white stripes painted on a road denotes a sanctioned place for pedestrians to use when crossing the road. Did your answers match up? It's very likely that others in your cultural community share the same understandings of these particular symbols.

Of course, context matters when we interpret symbols, and not only the cultural context. We also have to account for the setting, the other people who are present on the scene, the activities taking place there, and so on. For example, imagine that you were driving a car down a busy street, and on the side of the road you saw a person wearing a backpack and holding their arm out toward the traffic with a clenched fist and their thumb up in the air. In this context, the thumbs-up probably does not symbolize "Yes, sounds good," "I agree," or "Sure." Instead, you would likely interpret this particular individual's thumbs-up gesture as a request to hitch a ride with a passing vehicle. With the question of context still in mind, have a look at the symbols listed below and describe what each one means.

Symbol	Context	Symbolic Meaning
Rubbing your thumb and middle finger together to produce a snapping sound	At a public speech, an audience member makes this gesture repeatedly while looking toward the speaker.	
Rubbing your thumb and middle finger together to produce a snapping sound	In a group conversation, somebody makes this gesture once while simultaneously exclaiming, "Oh snap!"	

(continued)

Symbol	Context	Symbolic Meaning
Rubbing your thumb and middle finger together to produce a snapping sound	A patron seated at a table in a restaurant makes this gesture several times in a row while also looking around expectantly.	
a hashtag (#)	Immediately in front of a word or words on Instagram, as in #love	
a hashtag (#)	Immediately in front of a 10-digit series of numbers, as in #123-456-7890	
a hashtag (#)	As a data entry request on an automated customer service call, as in "Press the pound key. ..."	

For ethnographers of communication a particular type of symbol, called a **symbolic term**, is of interest. As its name suggests, a symbolic term is a specific word or phrase that expresses a key concept or an idea that is significant to a cultural group (Carbaugh, 2007a; Hymes, 1962). In other words, symbolic terms express something important about social life in the groups in which they are utilized. When ethnographers of communication study a symbolic term, they look for what is *special* and oftentimes unique about the term to the particular cultural group that is using it. They also interpret what the term and its usage signify about the group's culture.

For example, two ethnographers of communication studied the meaning and use of the symbolic term "professional" within the online community of LinkedIn users (Hart & Milburn, 2019). Consistent with the English definition of the term, they found that LinkedIn users associated the concept of professionalism with their work and careers. Beyond that, communicating *professionally* on LinkedIn requires being truthful about oneself and one's work-related experience. At the same time, however, LinkedIn users are *not* encouraged to be honest if that means being negative about other people. The platform's code of professional conduct requires that users be "nice" to each other and build one another up rather than tear each other down. For instance, LinkedIn users should endorse one another's skills; however, there is no mechanism for honestly critiquing other people's work or communicative conduct.

Sometimes ethnographers of communication study symbolic terms that only exist in one language and aren't really translatable. These types of terms are fascinating in the way that they express something unique about the cultural groups that have given name to them. One such term is "heaty," a health-related word used in Singapore, which describes a state of the physical body resulting from one's diet and other conditions (Ho et al., 2019). The ethnographers of communication who studied the term "heaty" discovered that it was linked with Singaporean, especially Chinese Singaporean, ideas about physical health, including what local people considered to be healthy or unhealthy (Ho et al., 2019).

Now you try. Google "words that don't exist in English" or visit this Babbel webpage on untranslatable words: http://www.babbel.com/magazine/untranslatable-01.

- What words stand out to you as particularly interesting or surprising? Why?
- What might it mean that such words exist in another language?
- What do you notice?
- What do you think is significant about this?

_____
_____
_____
_____
_____
_____
_____
_____
_____
_____
_____
_____
_____
_____

Here's another quick experiment. In comparison to many other languages, English has relatively few kinship terms; that is, words to describe family relationships. Take a moment to visit the following websites listing kinship terms in other languages.

Kinship terms in Hindi: http://www.omniglot.com/language/kinship/hindi.htm
Kinship terms in Chinese: http://www.omniglot.com/language/kinship/chinese.htm
Kinship terms in Javanese: http://www.omniglot.com/language/kinship/javanese.htm

- What do you notice about kinship terms in these languages?
- How do they compare to kinship terms in English?

- What might be the reason for these differences?
- What might be the result of them?

_____

Other symbolic terms exist across languages but can mean different things in different places. One example of this is the symbolic term "dialogue." A group of ethnographers studied the concept of dialogue across three different language contexts—Japanese, Korean, and Russian—and found many similarities as well as differences (Carbaugh et al., 2011). Across all three languages, the term "dialogue" suggested "exchange" and "social cooperation" and required "speaking sincere[ly] ... about one's views; and listening in a way that is open to learning additional information, including the emotions of others" (Carbaugh et al., 2011, p. 102). In all cases, dialogic communication went along with the idea of (more) "equal" and "balance[d]" (Carbaugh et al., 2011, p. 103) social relationships. However, the researchers found that the goals of engaging in dialogue differed. In some cases, dialogue was expected to result in consensus, while in others it was assumed to lead to social action.

Some symbolic terms are so commonplace that at first glance they appear entirely ordinary and unremarkable. With closer scrutiny, however, they bear enormous significance. Take the word "communication," for example. A well-known ethnographer of communication was exhorted by his spouse to "communicate" more with his children. This puzzled the ethnographer because—as he saw it—he already spoke to his children every evening when the family sat down together for dinner.

- What did the ethnographer's spouse mean by telling the ethnographer to *communicate* with their kids?

- Which of the following would count as *communication* in this sense, and why? Small talk, chitchat, real talk, blah-blah-blah.

- What are people claiming when they say that they *need to work on their communication with one another*?

- What is being offered when someone says that they can help you *communicate better* with your significant other?

Standard dictionaries define the English language term "communication" as the sharing of information, news, thoughts, feelings, opinions, and so on. However, as you probably realized while engaging in this short reflection, when North Americans say that they want *better communication* with relational partners, it means something more complex. In a now famous study, two scholars examined the term "communication" and found that its colloquial (i.e., ordinary, everyday) meaning in North American culture is *close, open, and supportive speech* (Katriel & Philipsen, 1981; Philipsen, 1992). This type of speech is often conducted one-to-one and generally involves sharing personal information, carefully listening to the conversational partner, and ultimately accepting their views (though not necessarily agreeing with them). In other words, when North Americans say that they want better communication with a relational partner, they mean that they want to engage in honest speech that enhances feelings of intimacy and mutual support.

Why Symbolic Terms Matter

When you are a newcomer in a cultural environment, studying a symbolic term can help you understand local expectations for communicative conduct, including how—according to local norms—you can and should act. One example of this pertains to romantic relationships. Two ethnographers of communication, one from the United States and one from Finland, studied two dating-related terms: "talking" in an English-speaking American context and "tapailla" (loosely translated as *seeing someone*) in a Finnish language context (Scollo & Poutiainen, 2019). For now, take a moment to reflect on the meanings that you attach to the term "talking," as in "we're talking," to describe a period in a romantic relationship.

- What are the goals of the *talking* phase of a romantic relationship?

- What kinds of activities do people engage when they are in the *talking* phase of a romantic relationship?

- If someone was in the *talking* phase of a romantic relationship, could they also date other people?

- How long could the *talking* phase of a romantic relationship last?
- What happens when the *talking* phase of a romantic relationship ends?

_____

_____

_____

_____

_____

_____

_____

_____

_____

_____

_____

_____

In their study, the researchers discovered that the *talking* (United States) and *tapailu* (Finland) phases of a romantic relationship were seen as a time for learning about relational partners, to see whether a more serious relationship was desirable (Scollo & Poutiainen, 2019). During this phase, during which interviewees felt it was acceptable to also see other people, activities might include sex or just spending time together. At the end of this phase, which had no fixed time length, the relationship might be taken to the next level. Alternatively, people might return to being friends only, or they might end the relationship altogether.

On a related note, another reason why key symbolic terms matter so much is that they express important beliefs about people's roles, including their status, responsibilities, and rights. Take, for example, a study on the coverage of Hurricane Katrina in U.S. news outlets. Hurricane Katrina was a devastating storm that hit the U.S. Central Gulf Coast in August 2005. Because of the damage caused by Katrina, over 1 million people were displaced, forced to leave their homes, cities, and even their states. The people impacted the most were predominantly people of color. An ethnographer of communication noticed that in Katrina's aftermath, American journalists and news commentators began referring to the people displaced as "refugees," to which there was a strong backlash. In an analysis of nearly 200 newspaper articles and letters to the editor, the researcher found that the term "refugee" was negatively associated with otherness, passivity, and victimhood (Edgerly, 2011). The term "citizen," on the other hand, evoked legitimacy, agency, and rightful membership in American society (Edgerly, 2011). As newsreaders argued, the people displaced by Katrina were Americans and should thus be named as "citizens," a term denoting proper respect and status.

Finally, it's not exaggerating to say that symbolic terms are powerful, and they influence not just people's beliefs but also their actions. Consider, for example, the symbolic term "rights," as in dues or entitlements ("I have the right to do this" "It's their right to do that"). What counts as a right, and for whom? One ethnographer studied a conflict between two communities—one Native American (Ashinabe) and one largely White—over the right to engage in fishing on public lands in Wisconsin (Hall, 1994). In this case, the Ashinabe community members saw "rights" as something that individuals could exercise only in relation to others. The Ashinabe believed that group members had to be mindful of their "social relationships and responsibilities" (Hall, 1994, p. 69) with one another; in practical terms, this meant exercising their rights while also being careful to maintain balance and honor. For the members of the White community, rights were solely the province of the individual; that is, "what individual people, such as Bob, Mary, and Pat, may or may not do now and in the future" (Hall, 1994, p. 68). This group characterized the treaties between the Ashinabe tribes and the U.S. government as unfair and organized protest actions that escalated into violence (Ina, 1990; Johnson, 1988). One key takeaway from this study is that it's very important to understand not only how different groups define symbolic terms but also how they make them actionable. Only in this way can we diagnose and hopefully resolve intergroup conflicts, especially hot ones.

Studying Symbolic Terms in the Field

You can discover key symbolic terms just by actively observing, listening, reading, and engaging with others at your cultural site. As you do so, ask yourself the following:

- What particular symbolic terms come up frequently?
- What terms seem especially important to people's lives?
- Are there conflicting ways that people seem to be using these terms?
- Are there any "hot button" symbolic terms that are causing disagreement?
- Which symbolic terms do you think would be especially interesting to study in the context of your site? Why?

Now, with your particular cultural site in mind, select one symbolic term to focus on, and write it in the box below.

The symbolic term that I will analyze is …

Ethics: Public or Private Data?

Data on symbolic terms can be collected in various ways, including direct and/or participant observations, documenting spoken or written interactions between people, conducting interviews, or gathering textual materials and other artifacts. Regardless of the data-collection method, the researcher who gathers and studies the data has an ethical responsibility to protect participants' privacy as well as the confidentiality of *their* data. Using the word "their" to describe the ownership of the data by participants is very intentional. Ethnographers of communication and many other types of scholars tend to view words as "owned" by those who produce them. For this reason, it is important to directly ask people's permission to collect data on their communication, particularly when their communication is considered to be **private**. If communication can reasonably be considered to be **public**, then it might not be necessary to obtain permission to use it. Nevertheless, with both public and private data, it is important to be cautious about how the data is used, as well as how participants are represented in any reports that come out of the research.

Reflect on the following textual materials—would they reasonably be considered public or private? Why?

Text	Public or Private? Why?
1. An email sent to you by a friend or colleague	
2. Posters displayed in the halls of a university dormitory	
3. A comment posted on a photo in a private Instagram account	

(continued)

Text	Public or Private? Why?
4. Materials handed out by a teacher in a class	
5. A discussion thread on Reddit	
6. A reader's comment posted at the end of an electronic newspaper article	
7. A company's mission statement	
8. A restaurant's printed menu	
9. A website's terms of service	
10. Signs carried by protesters at a demonstration	
11. Packaging labels	
12. A book, such as a novel, history, biography, etc.	
13. Graffiti on the outside of a building	

Answers: The first four items in the list would reasonably be considered private data, intended specifically for a particular audience and *not* for the public at large.

Fieldwork: Collecting Textual Artifacts

For your research on your chosen symbolic term, you'll collect some textual materials of your own. The kinds of textual materials that you collect will, of course, depend on your site as well as the particular symbolic term that you are looking at. You should be careful to collect texts that are nonconfidential and could reasonably be considered public data. What kinds of texts might these be, and how do they relate to your symbolic term? Brainstorm some ideas below.

Text	Relation to symbolic term?	What makes it public?
1.		
2.		
3.		
4.		
5.		

Having thought through which textual artifacts you might reasonably use to study your symbolic term, the next step is to collect them. The ways in which you collect each one of your artifacts will necessarily depend on what format they exist in. Artifacts that are already in digital format, like a website's terms of service, are very convenient to collect and preserve by using a computer and some of its built-in tools, like copying and pasting into a Word document or generating a PDF. With nondigital artifacts that can't be readily acquired, like graffiti, you can potentially capture digital photographs with a smartphone and then use the photos as your data. If the artifacts are printed out on paper, like restaurant menus or packaging labels, you might be able to collect them as they are (but ask first!). In all cases it's a good idea to create and retain digital copies of all of your data as backup.

Data Analysis

In analyzing these data, the goal is to understand what the symbolic term means to people within the cultural community, why the term is important to them, and what the term tells you about life in that community. Engaging in this type of qualitative analysis is not a cut-and-dried process, nor is there one right way to do it. For many ethnographers, data analysis is in fact an iterative process, meaning that they go through numerous "cycles" or rounds of scrutinizing their data; thinking deeply about it; and using their experiences, interests, and theoretical frameworks to make sense of it (Tracy, 2013). As you analyze your own collected materials on symbolic terms, you should carefully read and then reread your data, examining how people are using the symbolic term, how they are defining it, and how they are responding to it. Use the six guiding questions below to help you in this analytic process. With each guiding question, be sure to carefully note the specific evidence in your data that points to or supports your interpretation.

1. Look over the texts that you have collected. Where in the texts does the symbolic term appear?

_____

_____

_____

_____

_____

_____

_____

2. Carefully look at the places in the text where the symbolic term appears. What is the context in which the symbolic term is used? Does it seem to co-occur with other terms? If so, which ones?

_____

_____

_____

_____

_____

_____

_____

3. What information can you glean about the definition of the symbolic term? How is it described? What is it likened to? What is it held up in contrast with?

_____

_____

_____

_____

_____

_____

_____

4. When and how is the term used? By whom? In regard to whom and/or what?

_____
_____
_____
_____
_____
_____
_____

5. How do other people in the community respond to the term?

_____
_____
_____
_____
_____
_____
_____

6. Is there any discussion or debate among community members about the term?
If so, what is the gist of that discussion or debate?

_____
_____
_____
_____
_____
_____
_____

7. What assumptions are wrapped up with the term about communicative conduct, such as how to properly be a member of the group and/or how to properly interact with others?

_____

_____

_____

_____

_____

_____

_____

Write a Research Memo

In the space below, write up your research memo on what you noticed/learned about the symbolic term that you have been analyzing. This could include how the term is defined in your cultural environment and what makes this term important to people in the local setting. How is the local definition of the term similar to and/or different from your own definition of the term?

_____

_____

_____

_____

_____

_____

_____

_____

_____

_____

_____

_____

Check Your Work

To check your findings, show your data and your write-up to a classmate. Do they see the same things as you? How does their interpretation of the materials line up or conflict with yours?

Reflections and Recommendations

Before moving on to the next chapter, take a moment to jot down some of your reflections, questions, ideas, and recommendations on the work that you just did, answering any of the following questions.

1.   What were your main takeaways from doing this work?

2.   Did you make any "bonus" discoveries that weren't necessarily related to the main concepts that you were studying? Ethnographers often end up with interesting data that isn't directly relevant to what they are focusing on. Rather than throwing those data away, make note of them here in case you'd like to follow up at a later time.

3.   Did you have any difficulties or disappointing results when you did this work? If yes, don't worry; this is a natural part of doing ethnographic research and something that you can definitely learn from. Take a moment to reflect on any setbacks here. What were they, and why do you think they occurred? How might you avoid them if you were to do this work again?

4.   What do's and don'ts would you pass on to your future self if you were to study the concepts covered in this chapter again? What would you do differently, and why?

5.   What additional questions arose while you were doing this work? If you were going to continue with or expand this work, what would you want to explore? How might you deepen or expand your work?

6. What other placeholders, notes, or reminders would you like to set down for yourself here?

_____

_____

_____

_____

_____

_____

_____

_____

_____

_____

_____

_____

_____

Optional Deep Dive

► For information on research ethics as they pertain to online and digital spaces, see the ethics pages on the website of the Association of Internet Researchers (AoIR). In particular, the AoIR paper _Ethical Decision-Making and Internet Research: Recommendations From the AoIR Ethics Working Committee_ is a good place to start. It is available at https://tinyurl.com/y4a5tzca.

► See also the AoIR infographic at https://tinyurl.com/y37bob6q

► Other good resources on research ethics are:

  » https://tinyurl.com/y4jvkjfc
  » https://tinyurl.com/y2xbey2q

► For commentary on the power of symbols, start by visiting the Santa Clara University (SCU) Markkula Center for Applied Ethics at https://tinyurl.com/yxklx2a3

  » From there, try doing a Google search on a symbol of your choice, typing in "symbolism of [ ]."

Credit

Metacommunication

Definition of Metacommunicative Terms

Look at the terms listed in Table 4.1. How would you explain their meanings to someone who wasn't familiar with them? Jot down your definitions next to each one. When you are ready, check your definitions with a partner. To what extent do your definitions of the terms match?

TABLE 4.1 Some Metacommunicative Terms for "Talk"

Group 1	a) To bluff	
	b) To tell a white lie	
	c) To bullshit	
	d) To gaslight	
Group 2	a) To let slip	
	b) To open one's heart to someone	
	c) To say something straight up	
	d) To come clean	
Group 3	a) To talk down to someone	
	b) To troll someone	
	c) To throw shade on someone	
	d) To yank someone's chain	

All of the examples above are types of **metacommunicative terms**, which are words or expressions about communication. Metacommunicative terms are related to and can describe speech acts (Chapter 2) or speech events (Chapter 7); what sets metacommunicative terms apart, though, is that they provide finer grained differentiation between communicative acts (Leighter & Black, 2010). Take, for example, the metacommunicative terms in Group 1 of Table 4.1. While each of these terms refers to dishonest communication, they are not exactly the same; rather, each term describes a slightly different way of communicating dishonestly. The same is true for the terms in Group 2, all of which have to do with communicating in an honest way, and the terms in Group 3, which are all about bothering someone. As precisely as you can, think about how you would explain the differences—whether subtle or stark—between the terms in each group. Check in with a classmate to see if they agree with how you differentiate between the terms.

Now it's your turn. Let's start with a general category of talk: complaining. What metacommunicative terms can you think of that describe some form of complaining? Brainstorm as many terms as you can, writing them in the box below.

Look back at the list of metacommunicative terms that you brainstormed. What differentiates the terms that you came up with? Who might engage in each type of communication, with whom, and under what circumstances? For what reasons? In order to achieve what goals?

An important aspect of metacommunicative terms is that they go along with ideas about the value of communication (Castor, 2009). That is, metacommunicative terms are wrapped up with local beliefs regarding what types of communication activities are good/bad, effective/ineffective, moral/immoral, and so on (Carbaugh et al., 2012; Philipsen, 1997). Look back at the list of metacommunicative terms in Table 4.1. For each term, reflect on how the communicative activity is generally perceived. Is it considered to be a good, valuable, worthwhile, and/or moral type of communication to engage in? Why or why not? Do you and your peers agree in your evaluations of these communicative acts?

Now take a look at Table 4.2, which summarizes research done on eight different metacommunicative terms related to the act of complaining. Once you have examined the information in the table, answer the following questions:

- What surprised you about these terms? What piqued your interest?
- What did you notice about the purposes of each type of communication?
- What similarities do you notice across the terms? What differences?
- What patterns do you notice across the studies?

TABLE 4.2 Research on Metacommunicative Terms for "Complaining"

Metacommunicative Terms	Community	Meanings	Purpose, Use, Significance
Kiturim Katriel (1985)	Middle-class Israelis	To gripe	Speakers engage in *kiturim* with others from their in-group to express concerns related to communal, public life in Israel. It is a way to blow off steam. *Kiturim* also helps build solidarity and a sense of community between conversational partners.
Shit talk, crybaby talk Huspek and Kendall (1991)	Male industrial lumber workers in the U.S. Pacific Northwest	Shit talk is to speak badly about someone.	In this community, *shit talk* is something that people with more power in the workplace do to those with less power. It functions as a way to keep the less powerful workers down.
		Crybaby talk is a form of complaining.	*Crybaby talk* is a way that workers complain about their workplace situation. *Crybaby talk* is so negatively viewed that workers discourage one another from engaging in it and silence their own complaints, even when they are justified.

(*continued*)

TABLE 4.2 Research on Metacommunicative Terms for "Complaining"   *(continued)*

Metacommunicative Terms	Community	Meanings	Purpose, Use, Significance
Bitching Sotirin (2000)	Female secretaries working in an international management consultancy in the United States	To express anger or frustration about injustices	In this setting, *bitching* was something that the speakers engaged in at work, both openly and covertly. *Bitching* requires a sympathetic conversational partner and focuses on workplace injustices, especially those committed against the speaker. *Bitching* helped speakers preserve a sense of dignity and was also a way to avoid direct confrontation with the people committing the injustice.
Thou soo, aih auan Lee and Hall (2009)	Chinese Malaysians	*Thou soo* is complaining about something that the speaker expects to have resolved.	*Thou soo* is an act of attributing blame for a problem to another person. Speakers sometimes use *thou soo* to directly challenge the people that they view as troublemakers. In this way, *thou soo* can have a confrontational tone and purpose.
		Aih auan is lamenting something beyond one's control.	When engaging in *aih auan*, the speaker talks about a problem that they see as nobody's fault—it's just life. Speakers engage in *aih auan* with sympathetic conversational partners, who ideally listen and offer support. No resolution to the problem is expected.
Jammern Winchatz (2017)	Germans, German speakers	To whine about one's personal situation	*Jammern* is a way for speakers to unburden themselves of pain and discomfort, while also eliciting sympathy and understanding from a listener. *Jammern* is negatively viewed as a passive, even selfish, kind of talk, whereby the speaker focuses on problems rather than solutions.

(continued)

TABLE 4.2 Research on Metacommunicative Terms for "Complaining" *(continued)*

Metacommunicative Terms	Community	Meanings	Purpose, Use, Significance
Oplakvane Sotirova (2018)	Bulgarians, Bulgarian speakers	To lament, mourn, wail, cry	Speakers use *oplakvane* to share their frustrations about life in Bulgaria but without any expectation of improvement. *Oplakvane* helps speakers identify their fellow in-group members and builds a sense of solidarity within the group.

As the information in Table 4.2 illustrates, another key feature of metacommunicative terms is that they name *local* ways of communicating, ways that may be unique to particular cultural groups (Carbaugh, 1989; Carbaugh et al., 2006; Lee & Hall, 2009). Furthermore, because local ways of speaking are shaped by local beliefs regarding how the communication should play out, with whom, and for what purpose (Hymes, 1962; Lee & Hall, 2009), metacommunicative terms can potentially express something distinctive about how communication is supposed to function in any local setting. In other words, metacommunicative terms reveal crucial information about what types of communicative activities are possible in local settings, the local meanings attached to those communication activities, and the degree to which those activities are valued or not (Carbaugh et al., 2012; Hymes, 1962; Philipsen, 1997).

Definition of Metacommunicative Moments

"Meta-" is a prefix that, when attached to another word, means "about." As noted earlier, metacommunicative terms are words about communication. Similarly, metacommunication is communication about communication. Finally, **metacommunicative moments** can be thought of as occasions on which people communicate about their own communication or the communication of other people, including what communication activities are (or are not) occurring, what those communicative activities mean, the value of those activities, and the morality or immorality of them (Philipsen, 1997).

Ethnographers of communication have long been interested in metacommunicative moments, even if they don't name them as such. Concepts like "metacommunicative vocabularies," "social drama," "cultural moments," and "rich points," which are related to metacommunicative moments, come up frequently in intercultural communication and ethnography of communication research. One example of a metacommunicative moment studied by an ethnographer of communication is the Hurricane Katrina–related incident cited in Chapter 3, when people displaced by the storm were referred to as "refugees" in the mass media, and the public pushed back against this characterization, demanding that they be called "citizens" instead (Edgerly, 2011).

Another example of a metacommunicative moment analyzed by an ethnographer of communication is an incident that began at an awards banquet at a large American university in the Pacific Northwest. One of the people being recognized at the banquet was an outstanding student who had immigrated to the United States. Born in Mexico and raised in California, this student was being honored for achievements in his major area of study. As part of the proceedings, the university president made a speech, during which he said that in California the student had been "driving down the highway at 70 miles an hour in the middle of the night to keep ahead of immigration authorities because he was an illegal alien" (Philipsen, 2000, p. 218). In the following days many members of the university community hotly discussed this moment. Some people, including the student honoree, described the remark as inappropriate and expressed offense. The president said that his words were meant in a joking way; then he proceeded to issue multiple apologies, the format of which were also debated. Some questioned whether the community was right to criticize the president's remarks in the first place and whether apologies were even warranted. In short, the community was intensely engaged in a metacommunicative moment, during which they discussed—in speech and in writing—their members' talk. The ethnographer of communication who studied this metacommunicative moment found that particular rules, unwritten and implicit, were violated on this occasion. Namely, that "the author(s) of difference may not subject the subjects of difference to a speech act that reinforces an image of political illegitimacy of those who are so subjugated" (Philipsen, 2000, p. 226). In other words, people—especially those in positions of power—should not name others as socially, racially, or culturally different when that reinforces their status in an inferior way (Edgerly, 2017).

A third example of a metacommunicative moment relates to the issue of hate speech. A Christian pastor in Hungary published an article in a local newspaper in which he called for his fellow citizens to exclude non-Christians from the country's sociopolitical affairs. Did this constitute hate speech? What was it about the particular national, political, and/or social context that made it hate speech or not? An ethnographer of communication researched this metacommunicative moment and other similar ones to understand how people in a local setting (in this case, the country of Hungary) determined what constituted hate speech and what did not (Boromisza-Habashi, 2013). This research revealed that the definition of hate speech is very complex and rests on a variety of factors, such as who produces the speech, what they say, who they are talking about, who they are talking to, what tone they use, and the type of occasion (Boromisza-Habashi, 2012, 2013).

What all of these examples of metacommunicative moments share is a general sequence of events. First, someone engages in a communicative activity, such as giving a name to a group of people, telling a joke, or making a speech. Next, someone calls attention to the activity, effectively saying, "We need to talk about this talk." Various aspects of the communication activity could prompt people to engage in metacommunication. Perhaps it is the type of communication, like the telling of a joke in a moment when jokes are not sanctioned. Perhaps it is the content of the communication; for example, it might be acceptable to have told a joke, but the topic of the joke caused a problem. Alternatively, it might be the way in which the activity was carried out; for example, maybe the person giving a speech did not use the style, tone, and/or manner expected by the listeners. During such metacommunicative moments people may evaluate the communication that took place, characterizing it as good, bad, effective, ineffective, proper, improper, and so on. Different parties might respond differently, with different degrees of intensity. The key point here is that the parties involved feel a need to communicate about communication. As ethnographers of communication, we can observe, analyze, and reflect on this type of metacommunication to learn something about the people who are engaging in it.

Now it's your turn. What metacommunicative moments can you think of that are occurring in the public sphere right now? Who is involved, and what are the points of contention? Think of one or two examples and jot them down below. Then explain in your own words how and why these particular incidents fall under the category of metacommunication.

Why Metacommunication Matters

Studying metacommunication—whether metacommunicative terms or metacommunicative moments—has great practical utility. First, it can help you understand local expectations about communication, including what is considered right and wrong (Carbaugh et al., 2011). By extension, this can empower you to engage in communication activities properly by local standards. For example, when should you come clean and when might it be acceptable to tell a white lie? Is it ever OK to tease someone or to make a joke about them? What is the right way to give a speech for a particular type of occasion? In effect, analyzing metacommunicative terms and practices in a particular cultural setting can help you become an effective communicator there, if you wish to be.

Second, looking at metacommunication has diagnostic value in that it can help you identify and understand communication problems. For example, what was it about the label "refugee" that upset people so much when it was applied to people displaced by Hurricane Katrina? What values about communal life are violated if an American university president makes a joke about a student who has immigrated to the United States? How do people identify what is hate speech and what is not? What amends could or should be made in these situations?

Finally, examining metacommunication is a way to understand deep aspects of a local culture, including information about people's identities, interpersonal relationships, social structures, hierarchies, and power (Baxter, 1993; Carbaugh, 1989; Castor, 2009; Katriel & Philipsen, 1981; Philipsen et al., 2005). For example, characterizing a person who is calling out workplace injustices as a *crybaby* says something about power, including who has it and who is allowed—or not allowed—to wield it (Huspek & Kendall, 1991). Calling someone a *refugee* positions them a certain way in relation to nonrefugees, or citizens, in their society (Edgerly, 2011). To call one's talk a form of *bitching* reveals something about how gender and gendered relationships are perceived (Sotirin, 2000), and so on. In effect, metacommunication is "a way to talk more metaphorically about interpersonal relations, social institutions, and models for being a person" (Carbaugh, 1989, pp. 112–113).

Studying Metacommunication in the Field

Before you begin thinking about metacommunication at your specific field site, let's start with applying this concept very broadly to current events in your neighborhood, town or city, county, state, region, or even your country as a whole. What metacommunicative terms seem to be most pressing today? What metacommunicative moments have occurred recently? What metacommunication, whether terms or moments, is currently being discussed or debated in public discourse? If you need help answering these questions, try checking local, regional, or national news sources for ideas and information.

_____

Now let's get specific to your field site. What metacommunicative terms can you think of that are interesting, notable, frequent, and/or important at your cultural site? Brainstorm as many as you can, writing them below.

_____

_____

_____

_____

_____

_____

What metacommunicative moments have occurred at your field site recently? Describe them below.

_____

_____

_____

_____

_____

_____

_____

_____

_____

_____

_____

_____

Now look back at the metacommunicative terms and the metacommunicative moments that you noted above. Choose one that you would like to study—and that will be feasible for you to study—and write it in the box below. If you couldn't think of an example of metacommunication at your field site to study, it's no problem. In that case use one of the current examples of metacommunication pertaining to society at large that you came up with earlier.

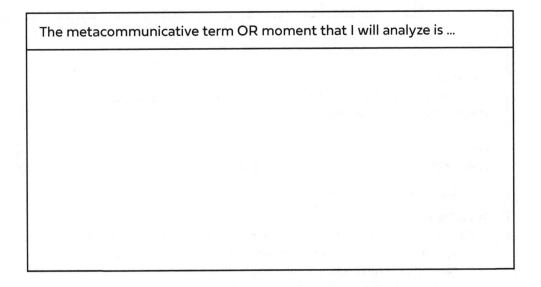

The metacommunicative term OR moment that I will analyze is ...

Ethics: Informed Consent

With any method of data collection, you have an ethical responsibility to protect participants' privacy as well as the confidentiality of their data. One step toward fulfilling this obligation is to ask for and receive participants' **informed consent** before proceeding. Informed consent means telling (i.e., informing) participants about the data that you would like to collect from them, how you would like to collect it, and whatever risks their participation might impose on them. Then, having informed the participants about this, you ask for their permission (i.e., their consent) to proceed. Only after they have consented can you continue, and of course, if they decline, you cannot proceed.

While obtaining people's consent orally is preferable to doing nothing at all, the best solution is to get participants' consent in writing. To do this, prepare a typewritten consent form that includes all of the information listed in the consent form template here. If you intend to audio record or video record the interview, this should also be included in the consent form. The participant is invited to sign the statement of consent at the bottom of the form. You retain the signed form and give participants a copy for their own records. Again, if a participant declines to give their consent, then you are obliged to stop at that point, and you should not proceed any further.

CONSENT FORM

Introduction
Briefly state what you are asking participants to do. For example, "You are being asked to participate in an interview on the topic of ____."

Purpose
Briefly explain why are studying this topic. If it's for a course requirement, then say so.

Procedure
Explain what you plan to do during the interview and how. For example, "I will be asking you a series of # questions. The whole interview will likely take about # hours/ minutes." You could also share some sample questions to give participants a better idea of what you will be asking them about. If you are planning to audio record or video record the interview, state that here.

Risks and/or Benefits
Be open about any risks or benefits that participants might incur from participating in your study. For the type of social scientific research that this textbook is guiding you to do, it's probable that there will be neither risks nor any direct benefits.

Confidentiality
Explain what you are going to do with the data that you collect. Describe how you will protect the data (such as where and how you will store it) and how you will protect participants' confidentiality (for example, by applying pseudonyms) in any reports, whether written or oral, that you produce.

Voluntary Participation
Confirm that participating in the interview is completely voluntary. Confirm that participants can refuse to answer any questions and can stop at any time.

Contacts and Questions
Tell participants whom they can contact if they have any questions. Provide a name and contact details.

Statement of Consent
I agree to participate in this interview and to the use of my interview data as described in this consent form.

Participant Name

Participant Signature & Date

Fieldwork: Interviews

To get the data needed to analyze metacommunication, a combination of approaches is ideal. For example, you could first follow the guidelines in Chapter 3 to collect textual artifacts such as announcements, articles, books, bulletins, magazines, posters, public dialogue, news reports, and so on. In this step, you might not yet know what metacommunication you want to study, and so you look for instances of metacommunication that inspire you to choose a particular term or moment to focus on. For example, you might scroll through a community's newspaper, listserv, discussion forum, Facebook group, and so on to see what particular metacommunicative terms or moments are bubbling up. Alternatively, if you've already found an incident of metacommunication that you'd like to study, then you can examine textual artifacts in order to develop your background understanding of it. This is the approach that was taken by the scholar who studied the incident of the joke made at the awards banquet mentioned earlier in this chapter (Philipsen, 2000). Although the scholar wasn't at the awards banquet himself, collecting the right textual artifacts on this metacommunicative moment, such as newspaper articles, letters, and public statements, allowed him to effectively reconstruct and analyze it (Philipsen, 2000).

In combination with collecting textual artifacts, you could also engage in direct observations in the field (introduced in Chapter 2), using those observations to create jottings (also introduced in Chapter 2) and then field notes (Chapter 6). Using the method of direct observation helps you document how metacommunication plays out naturally in real-life settings. This method was used by the scholar who studied the metacommunicative term "oplakvane" (Sotirova, 2018), mentioned earlier in this chapter. To study "oplakvane," a Bulgarian language term for "complaining," Sotirova (2018) spent nearly 100 hours in the field, attending public and private events, services, and celebrations to collect data on people's "naturally occurring talk" (p. 310); that is, what people really said and did in the real settings in which they lived their day-to-day lives. Doing these observations helped Sotirova see and understand how people actually engaged in oplakvane, when, with whom, for what purposes, and so on.

Yet another way to collect data is through interviewing, which is the method that we will focus on in this chapter. Like any method of data collection, interviews have both strengths and limitations. One of the great strengths of interviewing is that it can help a researcher gather richly detailed information from people about their own lived experiences, as well as their understandings, feelings, and beliefs (Spradley, 2016). Like any method, however, interviews do have their limitations. For one thing, while interviews can help you document people's perceptions, they aren't necessarily an accurate reflection of what people actually do and say in their day-to-day lives (Silverman, 2013). The most reliable way to know what people actually do and say is to document them actually doing and saying it in real life in what ethnographers call their naturally occurring settings (Silverman, 2013).

For this chapter, you will collect data on your selected metacommunicative term or moment by interviewing people from your cultural site. To start, make a short list of five people whom you could potentially approach for this purpose, writing their names below.

People whom I could potentially interview	
1.	
2.	
3.	
4.	
5.	

Next, prepare some interview questions. As you design your questions, consider what you are trying to learn about metacommunication. The analysis questions listed in the next section of this chapter can help you with this—just be mindful about phrasing questions in a way that makes them understandable and relatable to your interviewees. Know, too, that preparing for and conducting interviews is both an art and a learned skill (Spradley, 2016). As with all of the other methods covered in this workbook, taking a deeper dive into the method and all of its best practices is certainly worthwhile.

Interview questions about a metacommunicative term or moment	
1.	
2.	
3.	
4.	
5.	
6.	
7.	
8.	

Finally, conduct your interviews. For each interview, be sure to get informed consent. If someone does not give their consent, then don't interview them! As you conduct your interview, take notes on the information shared by your participants.

Although more detailed information on audio recording and video recording your data will be covered in Chapter 5, it's worth mentioning here that an alternative to conducting interviews in person is to conduct them remotely, using audio- and video-enabled meeting platforms such as Zoom, GoToMeeting, Google Hangouts, Skype, and so on. What's more, many of these platforms have recording options built in, and some of them will even automatically generate a rough-cut transcription of the meeting once it has concluded, which is extremely useful for doing your data analysis.

Interview #1 notes

Interview #2 notes

Interview #3 notes

Data Analysis

Now that you have collected your interview data, it's time for the data analysis. For each interview that you have conducted, any recordings, notes, or transcripts that you generated all count as data. The overarching goal of analyzing these particular data is to understand what the metacommunication that you are examining signifies to people within the cultural community. As always, engaging in the analysis is a complex, iterative process. Be sure to carefully look over your data as much as needed, using the guiding questions for analyzing metacommunicative terms (Table 4.3) or metacommunicative moments (Table 4.4) below.

TABLE 4.3 Guiding Questions for Analyzing Metacommunicative Terms

1.	How do community members define the term? What does the term mean?
2.	Who can engage in this communicative activity? When? Where? With whom?
3.	How is this activity carried out? What actions compose it?
4.	What is the purpose of the activity?
5.	How do locals value this activity? Positively, negatively, neutrally?
6.	What does the metacommunicative term draw attention to? Emphasize?
7.	What does the term say or suggest about the community's ideals; for example, what should/shouldn't be?
8.	What does the term say or suggest about relationships between people in the community?
9.	What does the term say or suggest about power dynamics?

TABLE 4.4 Guiding Questions for Analyzing Metacommunicative Moments

1.	What was the initial communicative moment that prompted the metacommunicative response?
2.	What was the substance of the metacommunicative response? What did people say about the original moment, and why?
3.	How did people respond to the metacommunicative discussion/debate? Was the situation resolved? If so, how? If not, why not?
4.	What does the moment say or suggest about the community's ideals; for example, what should/shouldn't be?
5.	What does the moment say or suggest about relationships between people in the community?
6.	What does the moment say or suggest about power dynamics?

Write a Research Memo

In the space below, write up your research memo on what you noticed and learned about the metacommunicative term or metacommunicative moment that you analyzed. What does your analysis suggest about cultural life at your site?

Check Your Work

To check your findings, show the write-up of your findings to someone from the cultural community. Do they agree with your analysis? If not, why not?

Reflections and Recommendations

Before moving on to the next chapter, take a moment to jot down some of your reflections, questions, ideas, and recommendations on the work that you just did, answering any of the following questions.

1. What were your main takeaways from doing this work?

2. Did you make any "bonus" discoveries that weren't necessarily related to the main concepts that you were studying? Ethnographers often end up with interesting data that isn't directly relevant to what they are focusing on. Rather than throwing those data away, make note of them here in case you'd like to follow up at a later time.

3. Did you have any difficulties or disappointing results when you did this work? If yes, don't worry; this is a natural part of doing ethnographic research and something that you can definitely learn from. Take a moment to reflect on any setbacks here. What were they, and why do you think they occurred? How might you avoid them if you were to do this work again?

4. What do's and don'ts would you pass on to your future self if you were to study the concepts covered in this chapter again? What would you do differently, and why?

5. What additional questions arose while you were doing this work? If you were going to continue with or expand this work, what would you want to explore? How might you deepen or expand your work?

6. What other placeholders, notes, or reminders would you like to set down for yourself here?

_____

_____

_____

_____

_____

_____

_____

_____

_____

_____

_____

_____

_____

Optional Deep Dive

▶ The University of Southern California Libraries website offers an overview of obtaining informed consent at https://tinyurl.com/y2s9kskd

▶ The University of Chicago Social and Behavioral Sciences Institutional Review Board has a number of downloadable consent templates at https://tinyurl.com/y58nbw27

▶ The University of Wisconsin–Eau Claire (UWEC) offers a downloadable PDF human subject protection guide at https://tinyurl.com/y28uqlyx

▶ It's worth checking to see whether your institution subscribes to the Collaborative Institutional Training Initiative (CITI) Program. If it does, you may be able to take their online coursework at https://tinyurl.com/y75sr3n6

▶ Harvard University has a downloadable guide on conducting qualitative interviews at https://tinyurl.com/yaltnbhs

▶ Anthropology Professor Emeritus David K. Jordan of the University of California, San Diego (UCSD) offers a guide on ethnographic interviewing at https://tinyurl.com/y3fl5mou

Cognitive Scripts

Definition of Cognitive Scripts

When you hear the term "script," what do you think of? The first thing that probably comes to mind is the written text of a theatrical play or film, used to tell actors what to do and say in each scene. This kind of script might be very detailed, laying out precisely how the players must read their lines, along with the required timing, emotions, expressions, and gestures. In other cases, though, the script might be less of a dictate and more of a general guideline for action, providing a series of prompts to help the actors navigate the scene. In either case, "script" is associated with performance, characters, lines of dialogue, and social activity—all of which are imagined by the creative team (writer, director, cinematographer) and laid out for the actors to bring to life.

There is another meaning of the term "script," adapted from the scholarship of Erving Goffman, a sociologist who researched everyday human interaction. Goffman (1959, 1963) used the term "script" to express the idea that in our everyday routine activities we play out predetermined roles associated with particular settings and the typical activities that take place within them. Take, for example, the act of eating a meal at a restaurant (cf. Shoemaker, 1996). The cognitive script for eating a meal in a restaurant generally includes the key roles of the customer, greeter, and server, and in many cultural contexts the cognitive script goes along following lines.

COGNITIVE SCRIPT FOR EATING IN A RESTAURANT

When the diner enters the restaurant, they pause in the reception area and wait to be seated. A restaurant employee will greet the customer and select the table for them, then walk the customer to their seat and provide a printed copy of the menu. Once seated at the table, the customer is expected to remain there for the duration of the meal; that is, they cannot change over to another table or another location within the restaurant.

Next, a server approaches the table and greets the customer, often giving their first name by way of introduction; the customer, however, does not give their name. From here on out, the main focus of talk between the customer and server is the menu. The server may describe any specials of the day or explain the items on the menu; the customer and the server do not engage in small talk or conversation on other topics. The customer may ask questions about the menu items and their preparation; they may also request modifications to their order. The customer may order drinks while deciding on their main course or at any point during the meal. Desserts, on the other hand, are usually ordered only after the main course has been finished by the customer and cleared away by the server.

During the meal, the server returns to the table periodically to ask the customer if everything is all right and/or if they need anything. Other restaurant personnel might also come to the table—for example, to refill the customer's water glass or replenish any "bottomless" menu items like soda fountain drinks, bread, or chips.

At the conclusion of the meal, the customer asks the server for the bill, which the server then brings to the table. The customer remains seated at the table while paying the bill. The customer decides how much to tip the server and either calculates that into the final bill themselves or leaves cash on the table. Once the customer has paid, they get up from the table and show themselves out of the restaurant.

The restaurant scenario illustrates the type of script that we are focusing on here; namely, a **cognitive script**. To say that something is cognitive means that it relates to the intellectual activities of thinking, reasoning, or remembering (Merriam-Webster, n.d.). Sometimes referred to by ethnographers of communication as a "cognitive map [or] schemata" (Saville-Troike, 2003, p. 20), a cognitive script is a mental model that tells us how to properly engage in different types of activities in particular environments. At a more granular level, cognitive scripts provide us with guidelines on what should and should not occur during the activity; which acts ought to happen in what order; what role(s) we are expected to play; what types of talk and/or actions are expected, accepted, and/or censured; and so on (Gioia & Poole, 1984; Hart, 2017a; Kivisto & Pittman,

2013; Shoemaker, 1996). In this way, cognitive scripts involve many key components that are covered separately in this book, such as speech acts (Chapter 2); norms, rules, and premises (Chapter 6); as well as speech events and their act sequences (Chapter 7).

In our familiar environments, we know the scripts for routine activities so well that they become intuitive and to some extent invisible. In other words, they are normalized and standardized to the point that we don't think about them. In fact, it is often through *violations* that our cognitive scripts actually become visible. Going back to the script for eating a meal at a restaurant, what if the server sat down at the table with the diner while taking the order or casually asked the diner for a cigarette? What if the diner walked back to the kitchen to pick up their food and carry it back to the table themselves? What if the diner tried to bargain with the server over the cost of the meal? Any of these actions—all of which would violate the standard cognitive script for eating a meal in a restaurant—would likely elicit surprise, confusion, annoyance, or possibly anger from the other players on the scene. In occurring, they would suddenly make the cognitive script for that routine activity apparent.

Think of your own experiences in public dining, whether as a customer, server, or observer. What examples can you share of communicative actions that seemed like violations of the cognitive script? What happened, and how did people respond?

_____
_____
_____
_____
_____
_____
_____
_____
_____
_____

The fact that cognitive scripts can be violated relates to their cultural aspect; specifically, that cognitive scripts involve cultural norms, rules, and premises (which will be covered in greater detail in Chapter 6) on what counts as competent and appropriate communication and what does not (Gioia & Poole, 1984; Hymes, 1972b; Saville-Troike, 2003). To a great extent, these cultural ideas are shared by members of the group to whom the cognitive script belongs (Saville-Troike, 2003). This doesn't mean, however, that everybody in a group agrees on every aspect of a cognitive script. Nevertheless, as with the other elements of cultural communication covered in this book, an ethnographer of communication would expect to see patterns and consistencies in cognitive scripts across members of a group (Philipsen, 2010b; Philipsen et al., 2005).

Check in with your classmates. To what extent do you agree in your classification of what counts as a violation of the restaurant script? Comparing your thoughts on this point can help you identify the degree to which your cognitive scripts are shared.

Cognitive scripts can and do vary between cultural groups, whether those groups are institutional, organizational, regional, national, linguistic, or otherwise. In this sense, they represent norms, rules, and premises that are unique to a locale. The script for eating a meal in a restaurant described at the beginning of this chapter, for example, applies to eateries in some parts of the world but not all.

Even within the same cultural setting, cognitive scripts are highly contextualized, meaning that they are tightly linked to the contexts (circumstances, settings, conditions) in which they occur. Consider, for example, online learning environments versus offline ones. You have probably spent years being educated in formal learning environments like schools, colleges, and universities. Because of this, you have a very well-developed cognitive script for how learning occurs in physical classrooms, including how a class session plays out from beginning to end, what behaviors are permissible when, and by which personae (teachers, students). What happens, though, when classes go from in-person to online? Suddenly, the classroom learning scripts that we are so familiar with might not apply.

This was the case at Eloqi, a virtual organization that offered one-to-one training in English as a foreign language—online only—from 2006 to 2011 (Hart, 2015, 2016). I used the methods covered in this workbook to do ethnographic research on Eloqi's teacher–student interactions, and one of my key discoveries was that on those occasions when the lessons did *not* go smoothly, it was generally due to confusion with the interactants' cognitive scripts for doing online learning (Hart, 2015). Predictably, technology-related issues proved to be an especially perplexing aspect of the cognitive scripts in play. For example, students had to join the lesson from a computer. Students didn't always realize that this was the case and sometimes tried calling in from their phones instead. When they did, the teachers were required by the company to end the call. Other technical issues arose once the lessons had begun. Sometimes, for example, the sound quality degraded, or the platform froze up. Whenever this happened, the students were supposed to hang up and call customer service. However, sometimes the students and even their teachers went against the script and tried to handle the problems themselves. Of course, in the period that Eloqi was operating, online person-to-person lessons like these were still fairly new and uncommon, and although Eloqi's teachers had received training in how to enact the required script, the students had not. In fact, many of the students were presumably learning online for the first time in their lives. Therefore, it wasn't surprising that for Eloqi's teachers and students, who were adapting their existing cognitive scripts for (virtual) classroom learning, it was sometimes a bumpy ride (Hart, 2015).

At this point, you might be wondering how a person knows or comes to know the cognitive scripts of any particular communicative activity or setting. The answer is that we learn cognitive scripts over time through the process of socialization; that is, "a formal, focused, normative form of enculturation in which knowledge and values are imposed upon the individual" (van Oudenhoven, 2013, p. 282). In other words, through our very membership and participation in different cultural groups, we gradually learn the norms, rules, premises, and expectations for doing routine activities there.

When we join new cultural groups, we use our existing cognitive scripts as a point of reference for learning new ones. Take, for example, the communicative activity of engaging in spiritual worship. Through extended fieldwork and participant observation in a Quaker community, an ethnographer of communication was able to discern a clear and regular pattern—effectively, a cognitive script—for the group's religious worship practices (Molina-Markham, 2013). Specifically, they found that this community's members engaged in joint worship through a series of discrete steps. First, they arrived at the meeting hall, where greeters shook their hands and welcomed them. Next, members seated themselves inside. There, the members sat in silence, "settling" (Molina-Markham, 2013, p. 135) in and carefully listening to their internal thoughts. If and when someone felt compelled to share their thoughts, then they stood up and spoke out their "vocal ministry" (Molina-Markham, 2013, p. 136) to the group. Then, at the conclusion of worship, participating members introduced themselves.

If you were a brand-new member of the Quaker community studied by Molina-Markham (2012, 2013, 2014), you might not immediately or intuitively understand the cognitive script for worship used in this group. Perhaps, though, you have first- or secondhand knowledge of how community worship works in other religious settings or other similar scenarios. You could draw upon your knowledge—basically, your own personal bank of cognitive scripts—as references for making sense of the activity. Gradually, over time and through observation, repetition, and practice, you would come to learn the (new) local script, and you would acquire the skill of enacting it smoothly and competently.

Why Cognitive Scripts Matter

Like the other forms of communication presented in this book, cognitive scripts encode deeply held cultural beliefs, so much so that when cognitive scripts clash, it can actually "confuse and disorient observers and other participants in the scene" (Provis, 2012, p. 59). Moreover, when people do not follow the expected cognitive script, other people on the scene may perceive this as disrespectful or even insulting (Goffman, 1963). This happened, for example, in a series of customer service interactions at a convenience store in Los Angeles, California, where Korean Americans were serving African American clientele (Bailey, 1997). The researcher who collected data on and studied these interactions observed that these two groups performed routine service interaction in slightly different ways. The service script followed by Korean Americans in this particular setting tended to incorporate just a short greeting, some talk directly focused on the business transaction, and a short closing. The script followed by the African Americans, on the other hand, included "expanded" talk like "jokes or small talk, [and] discussing personal experiences" (Bailey, 1997, p. 333), which served to foreground the personal connections between speakers. The different expectations that each group held for their service interactions led to misunderstanding and, to some degree, negative perceptions of one another (Bailey, 1997). In essence, the two groups experienced tension and upset because of conflicting cognitive scripts.

Another reason why cognitive scripts are so important has to do with their embeddedness in social, cultural, and economic systems. Just like all of the forms of communication covered in this workbook, cognitive scripts never operate in a bubble; that is, they can never be separated from the sociocultural systems within which they exist. To know a cognitive script for a given context is to know the expected code of conduct, and to successfully enact a cognitive script is to perform communicative competence (Goffman, 1963; Gumperz, 1992; Hymes, 1972b). When people encounter new or unfamiliar cognitive scripts, it can be very confusing, even disorienting. When people outright disregard an expected cognitive script, it can cause anything from mild annoyance to verbal and even physical violence. Furthermore, when cognitive scripts get laid atop contexts of tension or inequality, it can make those scripts even more consequential. For all of these reasons, learning about and being attentive to cognitive scripts is important, even when—or especially if—one chooses not to follow them.

Take, for example, the restaurant script that we discussed at the beginning of this chapter and consider it within the context of the global COVID-19 pandemic. During the pandemic, routine activities like dining out, buying groceries, and socializing with friends suddenly became potentially lethal. In a massive collective effort to slow infection rates, new protocols were instituted for participating in public life, including sheltering in place except for necessary activities, engaging in social distancing, and wearing masks in public. Rapidly, the cognitive scripts for routine activities had to be adjusted, and the common procedures for doing everyday things, such as walking into restaurants, ordering food, eating, and paying, all had to be modified. These society-wide changes to everyday, routine activities came with a lot of conflict and were further complicated by issues of race and social class, with people of color disproportionately affected by the pandemic and its negative impacts (Godoy & Wood, 2020; Nemo, 2020; Wallis, 2020). This was, in effect, a massive social experiment in—among other things—rapidly changing cognitive scripts. Public health as well as people's sense of selves, their feelings of community, and their beliefs about communication all hung in the balance. At the time of this writing, scholars had not yet begun to publish work on the pandemic from an ethnographic perspective, but this will surely be a major topic of research for many years to come.

Studying Cognitive Scripts in the Field

Think about routine activities in your environment, including ones that you directly participate in and those in which you are a bystander. These routine activities might occur offline in physical places, or they might happen online in virtual spaces. List some of these routine activities in the first column below. Then note the location where the activity takes place in the second column. For now, leave the third and fourth columns blank—we will return to them shortly.

TABLE 5.1 Locations to Study Cognitive Scripts

Routine activities that I often participate in and/ or observe, whether offline or online	Location	Public or private?	Could you ethically record people's interactions for this activity in this place? Why or why not?

Ethics: Anonymity and Recording

In the context of social scientific research, **anonymity** in data collection means that the researcher collects information about unknown (anonymous) participants (Lahman, 2018). This is different from **confidentiality**, which is covered in Chapter 7 of this book. As you engage in the fieldwork activities presented in this book, it is possible that you will spend time in public or private spaces where you don't know the people who you are studying—for example, a coffee shop, supermarket, restaurant, busy street, bus stop, train, or festival. In these situations, the question about ethically and legally documenting information about people's activities inevitably arises. How may you—and how should you—collect your data from or about unknown people who aren't necessarily aware of what you are doing? Even more specifically, can you create recordings (whether audio, video, or photographic) of unknown people without getting their informed consent?

In the United States, federal law stipulates that you cannot secretly record the conversations of people who have not consented. Further, it is illegal to secretly record "all conversations where an individual has a reasonable expectation of privacy" (Justice Information Sharing, 2013). That is, if a person is in a private place, and/or they can reasonably suppose that they have privacy in that moment, and/or they can reasonably assume that they are speaking/acting in privacy, then you cannot record them without their consent (Digital Medial Law Project, 2020).

In public places, on the other hand, it is permissible to "photograph or capture video of people ... even if they have not consented to being recorded, because individuals cannot have a reasonable expectation of privacy when in public" (Digital Medial Law Project, 2020). This "reasonable expectation of privacy" clause determines to a large extent when you can and cannot record people's interactions. For example, if you are at a political rally in a public place, you can record the speeches given by the presenters, who are communicating openly to the public without expectation of privacy. On the other hand, you couldn't record what two audience members were whispering to one another, since they would likely consider their words to be private. However, if those two audience members suddenly broke out into a noisy argument, shouting at one another in loud voices, then you probably could record them because their communicative actions no longer connote an expectation of privacy.

When it comes to video recording and photography, in the United States, "taking photographs of things that are plainly visible from public spaces is a constitutional right"; in other words, "in public spaces where you are lawfully present you have the right to photograph anything that is *in plain view*" (Annenberg Media Center, 2016). If you needed a powerful telescoping lens to see something far away, that probably would not count as "in plain view." When you are on private property, you must obey any rules about photography communicated by the property owners or staff (Annenberg Media Center, 2016). For example, if a restaurant posted signs saying "No photography," or if the servers there told you explicitly not to take photographs, then you would be required to follow those directions.

With this information in mind, go back to Table 5.1 where you listed possible routine activities to study and where to study them. Think about whether each location would count as a public space (like streets, public parks, etc.) or a private one (restaurants, businesses, someone's home), and write your answer in the third column. Would it be permissible to record interactions in each setting? Write your thoughts in the fourth column in the table.

Fieldwork: Recording and Transcribing Observations

Now go back to the list of routine activities at your field site and choose one that you would like to study. Ideally, the activity that you select should be easy for you to access and observe. For our purposes, it's best to choose a routine activity that you can feasibly observe at least one or two instances of. As you decide which routine activity to select, carefully reflect on whether you would be permitted to create recordings of the activities at that particular scene. Remember, you must always refrain from recording interactions that could reasonably be considered private, including conversations that you can't naturally overhear. And, if you are ever in doubt, err on the side of caution and do not make any recordings. In any case, you should always create your own jottings while you are engaging in your observations. If you are able to record, your jottings will provide you with supplemental information that will be helpful as you develop your field notes. If you are recording and something goes wrong with the technology, then your jottings will become your backup. And, if you can't record, your jottings will be your primary source of data.

When you do make recordings, then you should **transcribe** them; that is, convert them into text, before doing your data analysis. Making transcriptions from recordings is valuable because it allows for better analysis of the data that the recordings contain. Transcripts can be very simple, such as the sample in Table 5.2, in which only the speakers and their exact words are represented. On the other end of the spectrum, transcripts can be highly detailed and complex, with notations representing tone of voice, the speed of speech, and other vocal features like laughter, breathiness, and so on (Hepburn & Bolden, 2017). To see what the process of creating such a transcription looks like, visit Charles Antaki's (2017) online "Introductory Tutorial in Conversation Analysis," mentioned in the Optional Deep Dive section of this chapter. There you can view a series of four transcripts, which progress from very simple to very detailed. For our purposes, it's all right to generate simple transcripts like the one in Table 5.2. Just

TABLE 5.2 Sample Transcript

Annie	Good morning Stella this is Annie!
Stella	Hi Annie how are you doing this evening?
Annie	Uh very fine mm and uh this afternoon I tidied up my room and uh now uh my room looks more organized than before and-
Stella	Uh-huh
Annie	I feel very excited about it. *((laughs))*
Stella	That's wonderful, how motivating to work in a clean space, huh?
Annie	Yes ha ha-
Stella	Very-
Annie	that's very true
Stella	Very motivating, well good for you for accomplishing that.

be aware that creating even simple transcripts can be time consuming. Realistically, you should allow yourself at least an hour to transcribe a 15-minute recording.

To supplement your audio recordings, or if you can't collect any recordings, follow the process covered in Chapter 2 for creating jottings. As you do so, be sure to gather information on the following aspects of the routine activity that you are observing:

- What are the main roles that people play in this particular activity? Who plays them?
- What are the step-by-step actions that participants perform to engage in this activity? What order do the steps happen in?
- What kinds of specialized language (words or phrases) do people use in this situation?
- What kinds of rules or expectations (whether spoken or unspoken) seem to be in play? Did you observe any violations of those rules or expectations? If so, describe them.

Once you have left the field and are back at your computer, you can transform your jottings into full-fledged field notes, following the guidelines in Chapter 6.

Data Analysis

Now, examine your transcribed recordings, your jottings, and your field notes. Can you discern what the cognitive script is for your chosen activity? As best as you can, map the script out below, describing the broad strokes of the activity as it plays out.

_____

_____

_____

_____

_____

_____

_____

_____

_____

_____

_____

_____

_____

_____

_____

_____

_____

_____

_____

_____

_____

_____

_____

_____

_____

_____

Write a Research Memo

Now, in the space below, write up a research memo on what you noticed and learned about the cognitive script that you analyzed. What does your analysis suggest about cultural life at your field site?

_____

_____

_____

_____

_____

_____

_____

_____

_____

_____

_____

_____

_____

Check Your Work

To check the accuracy of the cognitive script that you identified, show your findings to someone from the community that you are studying. Do they agree with your analysis? If not, why not? What changes or additions would they make?

_____

_____

_____

_____

_____

_____

_____

Reflections and Recommendations

Before moving on to the next chapter, take a moment to jot down some of your reflections, questions, ideas, and recommendations on the work that you just did, answering any of the following questions.

1. What were your main takeaways from doing this work?

2. Did you make any "bonus" discoveries that weren't necessarily related to the main concepts that you were studying? Ethnographers often end up with interesting data that isn't directly relevant to what they are focusing on. Rather than throwing those data away, make note of them here in case you'd like to follow up at a later time.

3. Did you have any difficulties or disappointing results when you did this work? If yes, don't worry; this is a natural part of doing ethnographic research and something that you can definitely learn from. Take a moment to reflect on any setbacks here. What were they, and why do you think they occurred? How might you avoid them if you were to do this work again?

4. What do's and don'ts would you pass on to your future self if you were to study the concepts covered in this chapter again? What would you do differently, and why?

5. What additional questions arose while you were doing this work? If you were going to continue with or expand this work, what would you want to explore? How might you deepen or expand your work?

6. What other placeholders, notes, or reminders would you like to set down for yourself here?

_____

_____

_____

_____

_____

_____

_____

_____

_____

_____

_____

_____

_____

Optional Deep Dive

► For information on recording in public, start by looking through the Digital Media Law Project website at https://tinyurl.com/yxto6yvt. Although the site was discontinued in 2014, it is still an excellent resource.

► From there, visit the New Media Rights "Field Guide to Secret Audio and Video Recordings" at https://tinyurl.com/y2698wvx

► For more on the subject of transcription, visit Charles Antaki's (2017) online "Introductory Tutorial in Conversation Analysis" at https://tinyurl.com/yxnboljm

Norms, Rules, and Premises

If a teenaged boy is acting out, how should an adult respond? What if the adult identifies as a man? When, if ever, do you think it would be acceptable for a man to use physical force to correct a teenaged boy's behavior? What are some rules—whether spoken or unspoken—that would guide an adult's behavior in this kind of situation? What does it mean to communicate like a "real man"?

One of the very first published studies that made use of the EC approach was a research report that indirectly explored the questions above. "Speaking 'Like a Man' in Teamsterville: Culture Patterns of Role Enactment in an Urban Neighborhood" (Philipsen, 1975) is now considered a quintessential EC study of local communication practices. The author of this research article—Gerry Philipsen, the originator of speech codes theory—collected data around the years 1969 and 1970 in Teamsterville, a White, working-class neighborhood in Chicago, Illinois. Philipsen, a newcomer to Teamsterville, worked as the director of youth programs at a local community center. After starting the job, trouble arose when a group of teenaged boys began regularly acting out in a way that was "undisciplined, rude, and defiant of authority" (Philipsen, 1975, p. 16). Philipsen had to fix the problem, and he believed that he could—and should—use communication to do this. He thought that if he talked with the boys and engaged them in dialogue, then they would come to a mutual understanding, and the boys would stop acting out. However, when Philipsen talked with the boys, it didn't solve the problem. In fact, the problem just seemed to get worse, and the boys "became more rebellious and increasingly verbally abusive and disrespectful of adult staff members" (Philipsen, 1975, p. 16) at the community center.

For a moment, imagine that you were in Philipsen's shoes.

1. What would you consider a *normal* way for an adult male director to respond to the group of disruptive teenage boys?

2. What *rules, whether written or unwritten,* would you expect to be in place guiding or regulating how adults in this context, especially men, must or mustn't respond?

3. Why do you think so? What are your "deep down" reasons for answering questions 1 and 2 the way that you did?

Write your thoughts below. Then, after you have done so, share your thoughts with a classmate. What points do you agree on? What points do you disagree on?

```
_____
_____
_____
_____
_____
_____
_____
_____
_____
_____
_____
_____
_____
```

After his attempts to talk with the boys had backfired, a male Teamsterviller took Philipsen aside to counsel him on what to do. To Philipsen's consternation, the other man's advice was that Philipsen should "beat the hell out of [the] kids" (Philipsen, 1975, p. 17) who were acting out. Perhaps sensing Philipsen's aversion to this course of action, the other man tried to reassure Philipsen that he would even help out by "obtain[ing] the boys' parents' permission" (Philipsen, 1975, p. 17) for Philipsen to beat them so that he could go ahead and hit the boys with a clear conscience. Philipsen tried sounding out other community members. What would happen if a man tried talking with a misbehaving child instead of hitting them, Philipsen asked another Teamsterviller. The response was, "I don't know of that ever happening. That just wouldn't be natural for a man to do" (Philipsen, 1975, p. 19).

What surprises you about how Philipsen was advised to respond to the disruptive boys by the Teamstervillers, and why does it surprise you? If you were in Philipsen's shoes, would you follow the Teamstervillers' advice? Why or why not? Write your thoughts below.

```
_____
_____
_____
_____
```

_____

_____

_____

_____

_____

_____

_____

In the end, Philipsen didn't hit the disruptive boys. Instead, he stuck with what felt natural and normal to him, which was to use communication to try to solve the problem (more on this in a moment). As an up-and-coming scholar, Philipsen also noted the differences between his own norms, rules, and premises and those of the Teamsterville community, which figured into the creation of speech codes theory (Philipsen, 1992, 1997; Philipsen et al., 2005), which we'll cover in the final chapter of this book. Now we will take a closer look at norms, rules, and premises.

Definition of Norms

Communicative **norms** are informal "social rules" that tell us what we should and should not do in a given context (Hall, 2017; Hall et al., 2018). To say that norms are *informal* means that they aren't necessarily written down or explicitly spelled out. Rather, norms are accepted as "common sense," with the feeling that they are so obvious and such a given that they don't have to be articulated. This gets at another important aspect of norms, that they are *social*, meaning that they "are shared [by group members] rather than idiosyncratic to an individual" (Hall, 1988–1989, p. 24). Put differently, norms are what a group of people sees as the typical, usual, or normal behaviors. Because group members use their norms as the standards by which to interpret and judge people's behaviors (Carbaugh, 2015; Hall, 1988–1989, 2017), norms guide people on what they *ought* to do (Carbaugh, 1995; Hall, 2017; Townsend, 2009).

In the excerpt shared at the beginning of this chapter, the communication norm in play for the Teamstervillers was that hitting a person, even if that person was a teenaged boy, was a normal way for a man to (re)assert himself when challenged. If an adult male in a position of authority was disrespected and then used communication to respond, the Teamstervillers saw it as not just ineffective but abnormal, or downright "alien" (Philipsen, 1975, p. 17; 1992). For Philipsen, on the other hand, who had grown up in a different community in a different part of the United States, the Teamstervillers' norms didn't feel normal at all. Philipsen's norms guided him to talk with the boys, "reason[ing] with [them], involv[ing] them in decision-making, [and] understand[ing] their feelings" (Philipsen, 1975, p. 16). In short, Philipsen's norms went in direct opposition to those of the Teamsterville community.

This stark difference between the Teamstervillers' norms and Philipsen's norms illustrates how norms have two very important functions in our daily lives. First, norms serve as our guidelines for communicative behavior; that is, our norms are like a user manual that instructs us on the correct thing to do. Second, norms serve as the "standards" of judgment (Hall, 1988–1989, 2017) by which we evaluate the rightness or wrongness of actions. In this way, communication norms function as a "taken-for-granted moral code" (Boromisza-Habashi & Parks, 2014, p. 199; cf. Carbaugh, 2007a; Carbaugh, 2015; van Over et al., 2019). Every time we find ourselves asking what communication means (interpretation) or trying to decide if it's good or bad (evaluation), we are drawing on our norms (Hall, 1988–1989, 2017).

Let's pause here and practice analyzing the interpretive and evaluative function of norms. Look at the behaviors listed in Table 6.1. For each one, jot down how you would you interpret it; that is, what you think it could mean. Then, jot down how you would judge or evaluate it; that is, how good, bad, right, wrong, and so on you think the behavior is. Finally, try to articulate the norm that you think is operating in your analysis.

TABLE 6.1 Interpretive and Evaluative Functions of Norms

Context	Behavior	How would you interpret this behavior; that is, what do you think it might mean?	How would you evaluate this behavior; that is, how would you judge its rightness or wrongness?	Why did you answer the previous questions the way that you did? What are the operating norms that you are applying here?
An upscale, dine-in restaurant. The person in question ordered and ate a full meal then asked for the bill.	The diner pays their bill and departs without leaving any tip whatsoever.			
	The diner pays their bill and departs, leaving a 5% tip.			
	The diner pays their bill and departs, leaving a 30% tip.			

Once you've completed the table, compare answers with a classmate. How were your answers similar or different? Did you come up with the same norms or not? Did you feel that any of the behaviors in Table 6.1 violated a norm, and if yes, how?

Because norms are so consequential, when they get violated—whether intentionally or accidentally—conflict can arise (Hall, 1988–1989), depending on how strongly group members agree on the norm in question and how strongly they live by it (Hall, 2017; Hall et al., 2018). For example, when Philipsen refused to hit the teenaged boys and insisted on talking with them instead, the Teamstervillers viewed him as weak, effeminate, and not a real man by local standards (Philipsen, 1975). Nevertheless, Philipsen refused to change his ways and didn't hit the kids, and as time went on the Teamstervillers changed their view of Philipsen and came to see him as a saint (Philipsen, 1975).

Definition of Rules

Having discussed norms, we now turn to **rules**. Although the distinction between norms and rules can be fuzzy, there are some differentiating features. Like norms, rules are expressions about what should or should not happen in particular settings under particular circumstances (Carbaugh, 1987; Hall et al., 2018; Philipsen, 1992). Like norms, rules guide communicative behaviors and also provide a measuring stick by which to evaluate communication, judging how "appropriate" or "proper" (Carbaugh, 1987, p. 53) it is or isn't. However, whereas a norm has a feeling of "you ought to …" a rule feels a bit more like "you *must*. …" Like norms, rules may be unwritten; however, rules often do get written down, giving them a more formal, official, or explicit status than norms have. Similarly, the consequences for breaking rules may be more apparent, more structured, or more predetermined than the consequences of violating a norm.

Let's look back at Table 6.1, where you reflected on norms about tipping in restaurants. If the context that you were thinking of was dining out in the United States, then the norm that you articulated was probably something like: *If you eat a meal in a restaurant where you get tableside service, you ought to leave the server a tip in the amount of 15%–20% of your total bill.* This norm is widely understood and shared, even though it is largely unwritten. Breaking this norm doesn't have any immediate consequences and doesn't carry any penalties.

On the other hand, a rule at some U.S. restaurants during the time of the global COVID-19 pandemic was *no mask, no service.* During the pandemic, the Centers for Disease Control and Prevention (CDC) recommended that restaurants have their staff members wear masks, but it was left to state and local leaders to determine their own rules on the matter (CDC, 2020; Su & Secon, 2020). Some U.S. states, counties, or cities did implement such rules (Sabatini, 2020). On top of that, restaurants in the United States could choose to institute their own rules as well, and some did require customers to wear masks while dining in (Flores, 2020; Su & Secon, 2020). In those situations, if a customer didn't follow the rule, then they could be refused service (Baetens, 2020; Garske & Adan, 2020). On a side note, norms and rules guiding mask-wearing behaviors—not to mention their violations—were so hotly contested in the United States during the pandemic that they regularly made local and national news (Baetens, 2020; Flores, 2020; Sabatini, 2020; Zarroli, 2020). This suggests that the norms and rules for wearing masks during the pandemic will probably be a fertile area of communication research for years to come.

An example of norms and rules in recent EC research comes from a study examining a conflict among a group of academics in an online discussion group (Boromisza-Habashi & Parks, 2014). The conflict started with a *Wikipedia* page for a famous deceased scholar, where the people writing the page fell into an "edit war" with one another (Boromisza-Habashi & Parks, 2014). Their disagreement became so heated that one person (who was himself a scholar) made veiled threats of physical violence toward another, saying indirectly that he would beat him up (Boromisza-Habashi & Parks, 2014).

After this happened, the edit war became a topic of debate on an online discussion group where some of the *Wikipedia* page editors and many other scholars were active participants. Because the *Wikipedia* page interactions had devolved into "hostile [and] threatening behavior" (Boromisza-Habashi & Parks, 2014, p. 198), some members of the discussion group argued that the person who had made the threats should be shunned and all their past posts deleted from the record. The norm invoked here was that if a debate gets personal, or if someone attacks or threatens a fellow scholar, then the debate should be shut down and the offending person should be erased from the group.

Not everyone in the online discussion group agreed, however. Other members of the group argued that, despite the offender's bad behavior, the most important thing was to preserve the group's scholarly discussions. These members did not want the person who had made the threats to be shunned, and they strenuously objected to deleting his previous posts. This, they argued, would be tantamount to censorship or even "intellectual fascism" (Boromisza-Habashi & Parks, 2014). The norm that these group members invoked was that even if a discussion becomes heated, offensive, or violent in words, the debate must be allowed to continue (Boromisza-Habashi & Parks, 2014).

In the scholars' discussion group, the absence of any clear or explicit communication rules (Boromisza-Habashi & Parks, 2014) may have contributed to the difficulties in resolving the conflict. On many social media platforms today, the norm is that users can express their beliefs and opinions, even noxious ones. At the same time, though, these platforms often explicitly limit how far this free communication can go, with a common rule being that users are not allowed to make threats of violence against one another. We can speculate that if the scholars' discussion group had had rules like this in place, their conflict might have been more quickly resolved or altogether avoided.

Now it's your turn. What social media sites do you like to use? Choose one and, in the box below, jot down some of its unwritten but generally understood and shared communication norms.

Next, go to a web browser and do a quick search for that site's official communication rules. You might start by searching for its "terms of service" and follow up with "rules," "policies," and/or "guidelines." Write down what you discover in the "rules" portion of Table 6.2.

To what extent do the norms and the rules line up with each other? What do you find surprising, confusing, or noteworthy about these norms and rules?

TABLE 6.2 Norms and Rules on a Social Media Site

The social media site that I'm thinking of is …	
Some of its norms are …	Some of its rules are …

Definition of Premises

Having talked about norms and rules, we now come to **premises**, which are perhaps the most abstract yet important of these three concepts. Premises are defined as the communal beliefs and values that undergird people's conclusions (Carbaugh, 2007a; Foss et al., 2002). Put differently, premises are the all-important reasons—the whys and becauses—underlying norms and rules. What makes premises challenging to pinpoint is that they are so profoundly "taken-for-granted," "commonsense" (Carbaugh, 2007a, p. 178), and deep down in our minds that they go largely unspoken. In fact, we usually act on our premises instinctively, without stopping to think about them.

To better understand what premises are and how they work together with norms and rules, it's helpful to use the analogy of the Monopoly board game (Gopnik, 2017). The game of Monopoly revolves around real estate, and the goal is to buy up properties and force the other players into bankruptcy (Encyclopaedia Britannica, n.d.). Like most board games, Monopoly comes with a rule book that explicitly lays out what actions players may and may not take during the course of the game. For example, whenever a player lands on a property that is not yet owned, they may buy it from the bank. If a player goes to jail, they cannot collect their $200 for passing the "Go" space on the board, and so on. On top of these rules, there are unwritten yet widely understood norms about playing the game. For example, "nowhere on the Monopoly box does it say, 'It is forbidden for the players to use guns to force a trade'" (Gopnik, 2017); yet it's a norm that player don't use weapons to threaten one another during the game. In other words, some actions are simply accepted as norms for playing the game. Last but not least, undergirding all of the rules and norms for playing Monopoly are various cultural premises, which are the foundational beliefs, "values," "principles," and "unstated absolutes" (Gopnik, 2017) that we hold going into the game. For any given context, the premises can be numerous and variable. Possible premises for the game of Monopoly might be that competition is healthy, that each person must fend for themselves, or that it's desirable to attain as much wealth and power as possible.

Let's go back to a previous example that we looked at when discussing norms and rules, that of wearing (or not wearing) masks in public during the pandemic. As noted, there was intense debate about this topic in the United States during the pandemic, with some group wholeheartedly supporting the public mandates to wear masks and others vehemently resisting them. What were some of the premises underlying these two positions? Write your thoughts in Table 6.3.

TABLE 6.3 Premises Underlying the COVID-19 Mask Debates

The context is public life in the United States during the time of the global COVID-19 pandemic.	
For many people, the accepted norm—and sometimes the rule also—was that people in public should wear face coverings (masks). Why? What were some of the premises (foundational beliefs, values, principles, and/or unstated absolutes) underlying these norms and rules?	For others, the norms and rules for wearing face coverings (masks) in public were detestable, and they refused to do it. Why? What were some of the premises (foundational beliefs, values, principles, and/or unstated absolutes) underlying this position?

Another recent case in which we can analyze cultural premises is the Race Together public awareness campaign, which was launched by Starbucks, the international coffee chain, in 2015. The origins of the Race Together campaign went back to the death of Michael Brown, a Black teenager who was shot and killed by a White police officer in Ferguson, Missouri, in August 2014. In a detailed analysis of the case, the U.S. Department of Justice (2015) found clear evidence of "racial bias in the way police and courts in [Ferguson] treat black people" (Associated Press, 2019). Despite this, the officer was never charged, which led to intense protests erupting in Ferguson and elsewhere across the United States (Associated Press, 2019).

According to his own accounts, the CEO of Starbucks was very disturbed by these events and felt compelled to do something (Carr, 2015). As he put it, "If we just keep going about our business and ringing the Starbucks register every day, then I think we're in a sense part of the problem" (Carr, 2015; see also Starbucks, 2014). The Race Together campaign was Starbucks' attempt to acknowledge and address the problem. The campaign required baristas across the United States to write #RaceTogether on cups as they prepared customers' drinks. Then, if customers seemed interested, the baristas were supposed to engage them in a discussion about race (Carr, 2015; Starbucks, 2015).

Let's pause here for a moment and reflect on the premises of the Race Together campaign. In your own perspective, what do you think might have been some of the deep down beliefs, values, principles, and/or unstated absolutes underlying this campaign? Write your thoughts in the box below.

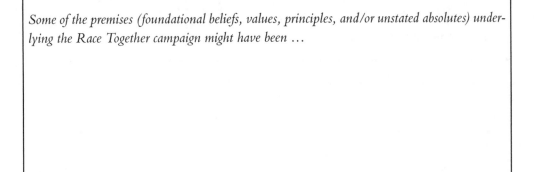

Some of the premises (foundational beliefs, values, principles, and/or unstated absolutes) underlying the Race Together campaign might have been …

Various premises can be argued to have underlain the Race Together campaign. One is that "race, racism, and racial inequality continue to be problems in the United States worthy of attention" (Logan, 2016, p. 104). Another is that words, speech, and open dialogue have the power to raise awareness, change people's perspectives, heal wounds, and even perhaps change society for the better (Logan, 2016; Starbucks, 2015; van Over et al., 2019). How about the premises that you came up with? To what extent were they similar to or different from these ones? What overlap do you see?

Before continuing with the story of the Race Together campaign, let's do some more analysis of the situation using concepts that we've covered so far.

TABLE 6.4 Norms and Rules for Customer–Barista Interactions at Starbucks

The context is Starbucks, a self-service chain café where people go to buy and consume beverages and light meals.	
Some of the norms guiding customer–barista interactions in this context are …	Some of the rules guiding customer–barista interactions in this context are …

Now, based on the analysis that you wrote above, how and why would you guess people responded to the Race Together campaign?

_____
_____
_____
_____
_____
_____
_____
_____
_____
_____
_____
_____
_____
_____
_____
_____

In many people's eyes, the Race Together campaign was a failure (Carr, 2015; Ember, 2015; Ziv, 2015). This was partially due to logistical issues; for example, people found it awkward and even impossible to combine the rapid preparation and distribution of drink orders with a meaningful discussion on race (Logan, 2016). But even if the logistics had been favorable, many felt that the topic of race was just too sensitive for customers and baristas to tackle (Logan, 2016), especially in a place (Starbucks café) and situation (customer service interaction) where the "unwritten policy [is] that you don't talk about politics, religion, and race …" (Carr, 2015).

What's more, among those who objected to the Race Together campaign, a key premise was that public talk about race would actually make the situation worse (van Over et al., 2019). From this perspective, public talk about race should actually be avoided, not embraced (van Over et al., 2019). However, whether people agreed or disagreed about its cultural premises or deemed it a success or a failure, the Race Together campaign was nevertheless impactful and important, since it caused a nationwide conversation about when, where, and how to talk about race "in service of racial equality and social justice" (Logan, 2016, p. 107).

Why Norms, Rules, and Premises Matter

Taken all together, norms, rules, and premises operate as a powerful force in guiding communicative activity. And although we can analyze them separately, it's still important to understand that they are very tightly intertwined with each other. Ethnographers of communication study norms, rules, and premises not just to understand and interpret people's communicative behaviors but to learn about their larger community culture (Philipsen, 2000). On a very practical level, this type of analysis can be essential when you are joining a new community.

There are some important caveats to studying norms, rules, and premises, however. First, although norms, rules, and premises may sometimes seem natural or inevitable, they are actually deeply connected to local histories and perspectives and often reflect a group's power relations (Robles & Kurylo, 2017). Who, for example, gets to determine a group's norms and rules, and who benefits from that? Second, even within the same cultural context, norms, rules, and premises may clash. As the examples in this chapter have shown, you can find conflicting norms, rules, and premises in the same group or community and even in the same context (Boromisza-Habashi & Parks, 2014; van Over et al., 2019). Sometimes, in fact, group members' disagreement about norms, rules, and premises *is* the cause of the conflict. Third, while norms, rules, and premises certainly do influence people's behavior (Carbaugh, 1995), this does not mean that people follow them blindly, without exercising agency or choice (Philipsen, 1992; Sprain & Gastil, 2013; van Over et al., 2019). On the contrary, people frequently disregard or challenge norms, rules, and premises and even deliberately flout them (Carbaugh, 1995; Hall, 1988–1989, 2017; Philipsen, 1975, 1992; Robles & Kurylo, 2017). Finally, a community's norms, rules, and premises are not set in stone; they can and do change over time

(Carbaugh, 1995). For all of these reasons, using the ethnography of communication to thoughtfully unpack the cultural norms, rules, and premises that we operate by can be an impactful and even a life-changing endeavor.

Studying Norms, Rules, and Premises in the Field

For this chapter's exercise, you'll choose a particular place connected to your field site and do direct observations in the field where communication is happening. Depending on your site, being in the field could mean immersion in a physical environment like a neighborhood community center, coffee shop, or restaurant. On the other hand, it might mean spending time in a digital or technology-mediated environment like a *Wikipedia* page, an online discussion forum, or some other platform. The truth is, you can study norms, rules, and premises in practically any type of setting where people are interacting with one another, no matter if the interactions are mundane or extraordinary.

Regardless of what the field site is, ethnographers generally engage in two types of observations in the field (Silverman, 2005; Wolcott, 1999). The first type is plain observation, where the ethnographer only watches what is happening. The second type is participant observation, where the ethnographer joins in the activity and also watches it at the same time. The reason that these types of field observations are so highly valued by ethnographers is that they allow us to directly see and make sense of what people really do in real life and why (Silverman, 2005, 2013; Wolcott, 1999). For ethnographers of communication, especially, direct observations help us understand *situated meanings in context*; that is, meanings as they are connected to people, places, times, and circumstances, as well as the cultural, social, and historical aspects of communication (Hymes, 1962, 1964, 1972a, 1977; Saville-Troike, 2003).

Ethics: Vulnerability

For any type of ethnographic research that you engage in, whether formally or informally, you are required to protect each and every participant and to be especially careful with any populations designated as **vulnerable**. Vulnerable populations are those needing extra care or support because they are more likely to be harmed—even unintentionally—by participating in research (Brule & Eckstein, 2018). In the United States the federal government stipulates that vulnerable populations include pregnant women, fetuses, prisoners, and children (Electronic Code of Federal Regulations, 2018).

However, it also bears consideration whether other populations might be considered vulnerable due to particular socioeconomic, racial, gender, and/or health-related factors and/or based on historically "[being] targeted with violence, hate, stigma, and isolation" (Lahman, 2018, p. 145).

Reflect for a moment on the cultural group that you are studying. Could that group be considered vulnerable in any way? Why or why not? Write your thoughts. When you are ready, share your thoughts with a classmate and get their input.

_____

_____

_____

_____

_____

_____

_____

_____

_____

_____

_____

_____

If you are working with vulnerable populations, you must take extra measures to protect your participants from any problems or damages caused by your research (Lahman, 2018). This means getting and documenting participants' informed consent (as covered in Chapter 4), anticipating any problems that your research might cause, planning out what you will do to mitigate any ill effects, and making sure that the potential benefits of your research to your participants are greater than the risks (Brule & Eckstein, 2018). For more recommendations on this process, read the guidelines on conducting ethnographic research published by the Research and Engagement division of the University of Massachusetts at Amherst at https://www.umass.edu/research/guidance/ethnographic-research.

Fieldwork: Doing Observations and Writing Field Notes

In Chapter 2 you were introduced to the process of creating jottings while in the field. Recall that jottings are quick, short notes, the purpose of which is to help you remember what you saw and did during your observations (Emerson et al., 2011). The main function of jottings is to serve as a basis for the creation of **field notes**, which are full-fledged and highly detailed accounts of your observations (Emerson et al., 2011). Transforming jottings into field notes is a demanding and time-consuming writing activity, during which the ethnographer goes through an intricate process of "remembering, elaborating, filling in, and commenting … to produce a full written account of witnessed scenes and events" (Emerson et al., 2011, p. 47). The reward of writing field notes is that you produce the kind of richly descriptive data that is required to identify and interpret aspects of cultural communication, such as norms, premises, and rules. This is nicely exemplified in the field notes below, written by Irma Campos, a student in one of my classes.

Irma Campos

COMM 154I

April 2, 2018

Field Notes #3

Participant Observation Date and Time: *Saturday, March 31 at 9 AM*

Field Notes Write-Up Date and Time: *Saturday, March 31 at 3 PM*

Location: *Sunpearl Community Farm ((pseudonym)), East San Jose*

It was a sunny, humid morning, at 9 am I headed toward the pavilion; there was no sign in table at that time. I saw Penelope ((pseudonym)) writing on the whiteboard in the middle of the pavilion. Penelope was wearing the light green Sunpearl logo T-shirt, jeans, and sandals. I asked her where I should go since it was my first time volunteering in the Farm Stand. She told me to follow her to the Sunpearl office which is a short walk away from the white building. The office was spacious with about five desks and lots of papers and boxes all over. There was an orange cat in a cat bed and many posters and trinkets around the office. Penelope explained to me the opening duties for Farm Stand volunteers. She gave me a training document then she opened the top drawer of a black cabinet in the room. Penelope explained that the staff members always had keys for all of the doors and locks and if I needed to use them I just had to ask her.

Once the top drawer was open, she took out a cash box, iPad, and an EBT card machine. We then walked back toward the Farm Stand, and we began to open the stand. I had never been in the Farm Stand, and it was decorated with dried flowers hanging from the ceiling, and there was a white table and about five chairs in the middle. On the right side was the register area which was packed with pamphlets, a cup of pens, some papers, stickers, and pictures of the farm animals and some facts about the farm. In the back of the cash register area, there was a black wall with a drawing of the Sunpearl site and a description of the First Saturday schedule and activities. There was a framed drawing of two red hens, and it read "Thanks for the eggs, ladies," this was next to the weight scale, and on the perimeter, there were brochures for the programs in the farm and those of the partnering organizations in the area.

The process of setting up began with us opening the entrance to the Farm Stand which is on the side and is the first building people see when they walk into the site. There was a latch we had to move, and then we slid the door to the other side. After that, we moved the white, wooden Sunpearl sign into the front and put it against one of the wooden beams of the Farm Stand. After that Penelope took me to the kitchen building. Inside the building, there were steel kitchen appliances and a long table that had stacked yellow bins on it. There was also boxes of fruit and vegetables on the table and on the floor there were three blue and white, long coolers which were filled with vegetables. Penelope told me to fill yellow, plastic bins with produce. There were red lettuce heads, artichokes, carrots, beets, green onions, fennel, romanescos, avocados, radishes, beetroots, and oranges. Penelope explained that the majority of the produce was from the Sunpearl farm, but some vegetables like the avocados were from another farm called Ginnybean. Penelope said that since some of the vegetables from the farm were not ready to be harvested yet, they worked with local farms to buy other produce to fill the stand. After that I began to move the produce into the bins and transport the bins onto the wooden racks which were outside the Farm Stand wall, this is where the fruits and vegetables were displayed.

Once all the produce was finally organized Penelope told me to wash the eggs, and she showed me how to do so. The chicken eggs were brightly colored like mint grey and orangey brown, they did not look like the supermarket eggs I buy. Penelope showed me how to wash eggs: first use a small washcloth and a bowl of lukewarm water, grab an egg and dip the washcloth in the water and then scrub the egg gently to take off any dirt or hay. The eggs also varied in size, unlike the uniformly sized eggs that I am used to. Some were tiny, and others looked way bigger than I had seen.

I was about halfway through the first egg carton when Penelope told me to go with her to the register so I could learn how to use the point of sale (POS) system and the basics of the cash wrap. She started with the iPad and let me know the password and the password for the app called Square which is used as the POS for the Farm Stand. It was also written inside of the cash box lid along with the correct amount of change there should be at the beginning of a shift. After that, she told me the produce that I had to weigh, today it was only oranges. There was a scale to the left of the register area, and she showed me how to weigh the produce. After that, she told me to read the training document so that I could familiarize myself with the POS system.

After about 10 minutes we had our first customer ask us for the prices of the vegetables. Penelope told her to wait a bit since it opens at 10 am. I began to put prices on some wooden tags and clip them onto some long wooden sticks. I then stuck the price tags in the holes on the edges of the yellow bins. ((I noticed that prices for particular vegetables were significantly lower than at the grocery stores.)) After I was halfway done the lady asked me if she could buy now and I said yes. She purchased about fifteen dollars' worth of produce, and she was very friendly and kept commenting that the vegetables "look very tasty." After she left Penelope also told me that there was a sign-in sheet for customers, it was used to email customers and it would be later entered into the system to help Sunpearl apply for a grant to fund the Farm Stand. The sign-in sheet asked for people's name, how many people they came with, their phone number, zip code and email address but the last one was optional.

It was pretty slow on the Farm Stand, so I looked over to the entrance and saw that there was a large group of volunteers, about fifteen, spread alongside the fence of the Youth Garden. They had weeding tools with them and wheelbarrows; they were working together and were doing so at a slow and steady pace. I noticed that they would glance in my direction at times. ((I felt a bit uneasy because I was in the shade while they were working in the heat, but I could not leave the post unattended either.)) After a bit we had two more customers arrive, they were two women with workout clothes and yoga mats, they asked me what time the yoga session would begin. I asked Penelope, and she let them know that the yoga was only on First Saturdays, the women laughed, and they made some small talk with Penelope. One of them told me she was going to shop, so I offered her a free canvas bag. She asked about the price for the eggs, and I said to her four dollars for six eggs. She took two dozen and then she looked at the produce and bought some lettuce, carrots, green onion. Once she was done I slid her card but it was not working. I told Penelope, and she went to the office to manually input it. Meanwhile, the two ladies asked me if it was okay if they could take a tour of the site, I said it would be fine. They went off to the see the farm, and I looked over at the weeding group by the Youth Garden, the people were crouched down low, and others were using shovels to dig into the roots of the weeds.

Penelope came back with the card, and she finally finished the transaction. After that there was a woman, man and two children who walked up to the Farm Stand, they were speaking Spanish, and I could hear them talking about how fresh the produce looked. The man stepped up to the register, and he purchased some avocados and green onions, he also asked if there was always the same vegetables and I let him know it depended on what was harvested each week. The lady he was with looked at the wooden shelf with the Sunpearl merchandise and she picked out a bag of coffee. She smelled it and smiled, and she paid for it, thanked me and walked away with the man.

Also, Penelope had let me know that the oranges and lemons and other fruits were harvested from the homes of community members and were harvested every Saturday by volunteers. Penelope told me people could sign up online to have their fruits harvested. ((I think that this is a perfect example of working with the community to utilize all the food available and distribute it in an organized manner. Many people that I know sometimes have no idea what to do with extra oranges and lemons, and sometimes these will just be wasted and thrown away.)) I had another customer drive up, she was a Park Ranger, and she was very friendly, and she knew the prices to the vegetables and she greeted Penelope. Penelope let me know that she always came by every Saturday to pick up produce.

After her, there was a lady with a young boy, and they asked me for a bag, I gave it to them and they began to examine the array of vegetables. Then they went up to the cash wrap area and placed their produce on the stand, she then showed me the Veggie Voucher which said it was worth eight dollars. I quickly read the training document to see how to process the voucher. I rang up the items, and it came out to twelve dollars, and she asked me to take out the artichoke, and it went down to seven dollars. I then circled the number 1 on the voucher to show that she had used it but still had a remaining balance. The next customer was an older woman and she was friendly and asked me to help her pick out vegetables. She studied the bagged lettuce and the red lettuce heads and asked, "Which one do you think is better?" I told her it depended on her taste and what she was going to use it for. She picked the lettuce head and I grabbed her canvas bag. She examined the Romanesco and asked me what it was. I told her it was like cauliflower but more green. I felt like it was her first time because she kept asking me questions on the types of vegetables and the prices.

At around 12:06 the volunteers who were alongside the Youth Garden started to put the weeds into the back of the Sunpearl truck. They worked together to carry the piles of plants into the truck, after a while the back of the truck was full. Some of the volunteers went on the back of the van, and they drove away. I could see and hear peacocks in the distance, and they would walk outside the perimeter of the Farm Stand every so often. ((As I looked at the group I thought about how I usually do not get a chance to observe the interaction during farming because I am farming, but this time I could see how people helped each other with lifting heavy materials. Usually, I am immersed in the fieldwork, and it is hard to stop and take notes, and this time it was a bit easier to take the time to observe people.)) There was a man who was older, and he would help people if they needed a wheelbarrow for weeds. He had long hair. I had seen him multiple times when I would be in the fields too, but he was never in my group. I think he has been here a while because all of the staff members always greet him and make small talk with him.

Once it was 12:30 pm and I saw that most of the volunteers were putting away their work tools and I could hear them gather at the pavilion. I listened to their voices clearly since the Farm Stand is only a few feet away. The people were laughing and talking loudly, and I wanted to walk over and watch them, but I had to take care of the cash box. After about five minutes I saw the volunteers walk out toward the entrance to the parking lot and they had bags filled with produce. I know from previous participant observation that the volunteers are given extra food at the end of a farm day. People seemed to be happy because they were smiling and observing the vegetables in their clear, plastic bags.

Once the majority of the volunteers had left there were only a few volunteers and staff left in the site. At this time, I began to take more pictures of the Farm Stand and the surroundings. On the left side of the Farm Stand, there was a significant cactus plant and small bush; this was a popular place for the peacocks to walk around in. The weather was also much sunnier, and it was pretty hot, it was bright outside the walls of the dark, shady Farm Stand. It was quiet in the room, and there would be the occasional noises from the roosters and peacocks. I walked over to the vegetables and adjusted them so that they looked good on the display. The vegetables that were first cleared out were the carrots and green onions.

Penelope let me know that I could take some produce home after my shift but she was going to an employee meeting for a while. While she was at the staff meeting, I was alone for the remainder of the shift, and there were not many customers after that. Since most of the volunteers had already left for the day, it was pretty quiet in the pavilion and the Youth Garden. I took the time to examine the pamphlets that were scattered around the Farm Stand shelves. One was for the Evans farm, another for meditation classes in Campbell. Another one was a helpline for undocumented immigrants, called a Rapid Response Network. As I looked through the brochures, I also began to read the training document on all the closing duties.

I waited for Penelope to be finished so I could start putting away the vegetables. Once she was finished, she told me to take all the price tags off the bins. Penelope then told me to write down the weight of each vegetable type as she weighed them on the scale. Once these were all weighed, she told me to count the cash, and she went to the office to log in to the Square website to print out the totals. Once I calculated the cash, I wrote down the total in the log in binder, and I waited for Penelope to come back. After about ten minutes she came back, and we proceed to put away the yellow bins into the packing shed where all the excess produce and eggs were stored. Penelope let me know that once the fresh eggs are washed they had to be used or they would go bad. After we were done with that task we walked over to the office to put away the iPad, cash box, and EBT card machine. After Penelope locked up the top drawer, we went back out to lock up the Farm Stand. We put way the Sunpearl wooden logo and placed it inside, and we put away the two whiteboards into the Farm Stand. Once this was done Penelope locked up the Farm Stand and we walked toward the office again.

((I think my experience as a volunteer at the Farm Stand was distinctly different than my past experiences when I am farming. I felt that while I was able to observe more, I did also feel guilty for not being able to help out as much. I mentioned this to Penelope, and she said she was working on making a plan for Farm Stand volunteers to have more tasks since this was not the first time that a volunteer had mentioned this to her. What I was able to do in this participant observation was examine the routines of the staff, in particular, Penelope, and all that she does to make sure the Farm Stand is staffed, filled with produce, and customers are helped.))

There is not one right way to produce field notes from jottings; however, there are some tried and tested guidelines that are helpful to follow. One is that you should develop your field notes as soon as you can, preferably the same day that you created your original jottings (Emerson et al., 2011). The reason for this is that, with each passing day, you will likely forget more and more of the details of what you saw and did in the field. Another guideline is that you should bracket your personal commentary in your field notes, which means demarcating it from descriptions of your observations. In Irma's field notes, you can see that she did this by placing her commentaries within double parentheses (( )). Finally, you should focus on "how members themselves characterize and describe [the] particular activities, events, and groups" that you are observing (Emerson et al., 2011, p. 136; cf. Hymes, 1962, 1964). Not only is this consistent with the interpretive paradigm to which EC belongs, it is also the main goal of EC work, which is to understand the world from the perspective of those living it.

Data Analysis

To analyze any evidence of norms, rules, and premises in your data set, use the following guidelines.

- Look for patterns in the data; that is, repeated occurrences rather than just a one-off event.

- Moments of conflict can be very useful for discovering and understanding norms, rules, and premises (Carbaugh, 1987; Hymes, 1962; Saville-Troike, 2003). Did you observe or experience any such moments? If so, what might they reveal about local norms, rules, and/or premises? If you didn't observe any conflict, no problem! There are still going to be norms, rules, and premises operating in the context where you did your observations.

- Be attentive to how locals evaluate communication; that is, what they consider to be good, correct, and/or proper communication versus bad, wrong, and/or inappropriate communication.

- Be attentive to what people say about the "rights and obligations" (Carbaugh, 1995, p. 285; 2007a) of group members; that is, how they are supposed to communicate and how they explain this.

- Finally, as you begin to identify norms, rules, and premises, try to put them into words as accurately and succinctly as you can for the particular context that you were observing.

Use the table below to describe what you found out about norms, rules, and premises from your field observations. Try to include some evidence from your field notes as a way of supporting the claims that you are making. Your evidence could be drawn from something that you saw people do or heard them say, or it could be based on other observations that you made and documented in your field notes.

The specific context where I did my observations was …	
A norm in that setting is …	Some (related) rules in that setting are …
Some data/evidence/examples that I found of this are …	Some data/evidence/examples that I found of this are …
Some underlying premises here are …	
I think so because …	

Write a Research Memo

Now, in the space below, write up a research memo on what you noticed and learned about the norms, rules, and premises that you looked at in your particular field site, in the specific context that you selected. What might your observations suggest or reveal about cultural life there?

_____

_____

_____

_____

_____

_____

_____

_____

_____

_____

_____

_____

Check Your Work

Do members of the cultural group that you are studying agree with your analysis? Share what you have observed with one or more people in the group to get their feedback. To what extent do they agree with your discoveries? Are there any points that they would adjust to make them more accurate? How?

_____

_____

_____

_____

_____

_____

_____

Reflections and Recommendations

Before moving on to the next chapter, take a moment to jot down some of your reflections, questions, ideas, and recommendations on the work that you just did, answering any of the following questions.

1. What were your main takeaways from doing this work?

2. Did you make any "bonus" discoveries that weren't necessarily related to the main concepts that you were studying? Ethnographers often end up with interesting data that isn't directly relevant to what they are focusing on. Rather than throwing those data away, make note of them here in case you'd like to follow up at a later time.

3. Did you have any difficulties or disappointing results when you did this work? If yes, don't worry; this is a natural part of doing ethnographic research and something that you can definitely learn from. Take a moment to reflect on any setbacks here. What were they, and why do you think they occurred? How might you avoid them if you were to do this work again?

4. What do's and don'ts would you pass on to your future self if you were to study the concepts covered in this chapter again? What would you do differently, and why?

5. What additional questions arose while you were doing this work? If you were going to continue with or expand this work, what would you want to explore? How might you deepen or expand your work?

6. What other placeholders, notes, or reminders would you like to set down for yourself here?

_____

_____

_____

_____

_____

_____

_____

_____

_____

_____

_____

Optional Deep Dive

▶ For additional guidelines on writing field notes, see the Writing Field Notes guide at https://tinyurl.com/y4jeg8m5

▶ As noted earlier, the guidelines on conducting ethnographic research published by the Research and Engagement division of the University of Massachusetts at Amherst at https://tinyurl.com/yxc78fnn are an excellent resource for how to protect human subjects.

▶ For more information on vulnerability, including the potential vulnerability of ethnographers in the field, see the New Ethnographer website at https://tinyurl.com/y2bhtsej

Speech Events

Definition of Speech Events

One time each year, a special town meeting is held in Amherst, Massachusetts, the goal of which is for the attending citizens to approve their town's budget. These meetings, which are highly structured and formalized, have been closely studied by an EC scholar (Townsend, 2009), who carefully documented exactly how they play out. First, as the scholar observed, the meeting begins with a call to order. This is followed by introductions, a swearing in of the moderator, and announcements. Next, a series of town-specific issues, like zoning bylaws, building signage, and so on, are presented for discussion and debate. For each new issue, there is an introduction followed by people presenting points and arguments in favor of it. Then all attendees are invited to speak out and can share their views either for or against the issue. Finally, after everyone's views have been heard and considered, the group votes on each issue.

Taken piece by piece, there are numerous distinct communication activities that happen during the Amherst town meeting, including the following:

1. calling the group to order

2. introducing key participants

3. swearing in the moderator

4. making announcements

5. presenting the issues

6. discussing the pros and cons of the issues

7. taking a vote on each issue

Each one of these separate activities could be classified as a *speech act*, as described in Chapter 2 of this book. When taken all together, however, these acts make up something larger—specifically, a **speech event**.

Speech events can be thought of as communicative *occasions* or *activities* (Hymes, 1974). Despite their name, however, speech events don't actually have to be "spoken" in the literal sense; "speech" is synonymous with "communication," so speech events can take many forms. Some speech events might indeed be carried out vocally in face-to-face settings, like meetings for worship (Molina-Markham, 2013). Other speech events might be remote, text based, or technology mediated, just like the speech event of *tokbek* (Dori-Hacohen & Shavit, 2013). *Tokbek*, a Hebrew-language term derived from the English expression "talk back," is the name given to discussions that happen in online discussion forums attached to Israeli journalistic websites. Through *tokbek*, posters engage with other readers and commentators as they respond to online news and commentary. This speech event involves the acts of making political statements, condemning the "other" side, and trading insults back and forth, all of which happens via written messages posted on the sites.

Regardless of their form, speech events are always composed of "a unified set of components" (Saville-Troike, 2003, p. 23). What this means is that speech events are generally made up of multiple speech acts linked or chained together in a particular sequence (Hymes, 1972a, 1974; Keating, 2001), just as in the Amherst town meeting example (Townsend, 2009). Related to this, speech events are ordered with a beginning, middle, and end (Keating, 2001; Saville-Troike, 2003), so when we study a particular speech event, we should be able to discern where and at what point in time it begins and concludes. With some speech events, like the Amherst town meetings (Townsend, 2009), discerning the structure and the sequencing of the events is straightforward because they are so highly planned and tightly organized. With other speech events, like *tokbek*, this may be a bit more difficult, since they are quite loosely structured and spontaneous. Related to this, some speech events are scheduled in advance, like "going up there," a presentational speaking activity in a U.S. seventh-grade social studies class (Bunch, 2009). Others happen completely spontaneously, like the American Christian fundamentalist practice of sharing one's testimony (Ward, 2010) or the Quaker practice of vocal ministry, in which members share messages from God with their fellow congregants (Molina-Markham, 2013).

The SPEAKING Heuristic

Speech events can comprise any of the elements covered in this book. For example, they can be made up of speech acts (Chapter 2) chained together; they can include symbolic or metacommunicative terms (Chapters 3 and 4, respectively); like cognitive scripts (Chapter 5), speech events can revolve around routinized communication; and finally, speech events are most certainly governed by norms, rules, and premises (Chapter 6). Given their complexity, it is very important to look at speech events holistically, considering how all of their varied parts work together.

To this end, the originator of the EC framework created a useful device called the **SPEAKING heuristic** (Hymes, 1964, 1972a; cf. Keating, 2001; Noy, 2017; Saville-Troike, 2003). The word *heuristic* comes from the Greek term for "find" and means a tool for discovering or learning something. The SPEAKING heuristic is a simple but highly effective tool, specifically for organizing and analyzing data on speech events. Each of the letters in its name (S-P-E-A-K-I-N-G) represents an aspect of a speech event that should be observed, described, and analyzed, as described in more detail below.

S: Setting or Scene

The setting or scene of a speech event refers to the place where it happens. This might be a physical place like a meeting hall, a university classroom, a café, and so on. Alternatively, because communication is not limited to physical places, the setting could just as easily be an online or technology-mediated space, such as the comments area of a YouTube video, an online discussion forum like Reddit, a Facebook page, a LinkedIn group, and so on.

When documenting the setting of a speech event, whether it is a technology-mediated space or a physical one, you should make note of its relevant features, such as the location; temporal conditions (hour, day, month, season); physical or spatial conditions, such as the layout of the space and/or how people or things are situated within it; and key movement or action of people or things, such as how participants arrive and depart. The setting's spatial design and its affordances and constraints can all shape the way that the speech event plays out; this is true for technology-mediated and virtual spaces just as much as it is for physical ones (Hart, 2015; Herring, 2007).

P: Participants

Who counts as a "participant" in a speech event? The most obvious participants are those who are visibly or volubly communicating; for example, in a speech event like a classroom lesson, the first participants that you notice might be those who are lecturing, asking and answering questions, and giving instructions. However, it's also important to acknowledge those participants who are present on the scene and whose engagement may be less visible or more silent yet is still legitimate (Lave & Wenger, 1991). For our purposes, then, think of the participants as all of the people who are present at the speech event, whether they are speakers, listeners, observers, bystanders, or lurkers.

Besides documenting who is participating—in any capacity—it's also helpful to note the roles that the participants play in the speech event, as well as their relationships to one another.

E: Ends

The ends of a speech event are its purposes and intended or desired goals. This could include the ends as perceived by the group, as well as the individual ends that each participant may have. Sometimes the ends might be expressed very directly and explicitly and therefore may be easy for you to pick up as an observer. At other times the ends might be only implicitly communicated, meaning that you have to carefully read between the lines in order to detect them (Fitch & Sanders, 1994).

In addition to the ends (goals) of the speech event, it's also important to note the actual outcomes, which are what actually happens, or the real consequences of the event. Put differently, the ends are what people *hope* will happen, whereas the outcomes are what actually *does* happen. For example, the ends of a customer service interaction might be to persuade the customer to make a purchase and to make the customer feel satisfied. The outcomes, on the other hand, are whether the customer actually does make a purchase or does leave the interaction feeling satisfied with the service that they received.

A: Act Sequence

The act sequence refers to how the speech event is ordered; that is, what happens when, in what arrangement.

To document the act sequence, you should make note of all the components of the speech event, as well as the sequence in which the components occur. In other words, what do the participants do, and when? What happens first, second, third, and so on? How does the speech event play out? For example, when eating a meal in a restaurant, it's customary to order and eat the main course *before* ordering a dessert. Similarly, one generally pays the bill after finishing the meal, not before. Although it may seem mundane, the order in which things happen is actually very important, as we know from looking at cognitive scripts in Chapter 5 of this book; hence the value in documenting the act sequence of a speech event.

K: Key

The key refers to the emotional tone (Saville-Troike, 2003) of the speech event; that is, the "tone, manner, or spirit in which [it] is done" (Hymes, 1972a, p. 62). This could include the "degree of seriousness, formality, contentiousness, and cooperation" (Herring, 2007) of the speech event, or any other palpable feelings being expressed at the speech event.

As you explore a speech event's key or tone, it's important to keep in mind that it can be highly subjective. In fact, different participants on the scene may perceive different tones at the same moment. For example, what one person finds funny another might find insulting. It's also possible that the key will shift and change as the event plays out. For these reasons, documenting the key of the speech event can be challenging. To the best of your ability, avoid guessing what the key is. Instead, collect concrete evidence about participants' perceptions, noting what they say and do. If possible, conduct some on-the-spot interviews to ask people directly about their perceptions of the key/tone of the event.

I: Instrumentalities

The instrumentalities of the speech event are the forms that the communication takes. For example, with some speech events the communication may be enacted orally, with people speaking to one another. In other speech events the communication may be enacted textually, with people composing and posting messages in writing. With some speech events the activity might be occurring in real time, at the same moment (synchronously), as in a live meeting. With other speech events there may be time in between the communication, as in an online discussion forum. Even more complex, some speech events may blend instrumentalities. For example, you might have one that takes place on an online platform, such as Zoom, where people are using oral, written, and gestural communication with one another, all at the same time.

Instrumentalities can also include people's language variety and style (Keating, 2001), a broad category that includes many things, such as the degree of formality/informality in a person's communication, their use of dialects, technical or specialized terms, and even slang. For example, a researcher who studied the reality show *RuPaul's Drag Race* found specialized terms in this localized context, like "fishy," meaning "girly," and "hungry," meaning competitive (Simmons, 2014). Other researchers have studied the development of specialized symbols and dialects in technology-mediated communication, like the use of emojis (Dainas & Herring, forthcoming).

N: Norms

As you know from Chapter 6 of this book, norms are informal "social rules" that tell people what they should and should not do in a given context (Hall, 2017; Hall et al., 2018; Saville-Troike, 2003). Their inclusion in the SPEAKING heuristic confirms that when you are studying a speech event, you should explore what the spoken and unspoken norms of the situation are. Furthermore, although rules and premises aren't explicitly named in SPEAKING, it is still worthwhile to identify them too, since they always exist in combination with norms. As you analyze norms, rules, and premises, follow the guidance presented in Chapter 6 to unpack both their interpretive and evaluative functions.

G: Genre

Genre refers to the type or category of communication that the speech event falls under. Some examples of genres are political speeches (Philipsen, 1986) and debates; celebratory speeches (Philipsen, 2000); public speaking in general (Boromisza-Habashi & Reinig,

2018); jokes (Fine & De Soucey, 2005); town meetings (Townsend, 2009) and other types of public and private meetings (Baxter, 1993; Castor, 2009; Leighter & Black, 2010; Leighter & Castor, 2009; Sprain & Boromisza-Habashi, 2012); discussion forums (Boromisza-Habashi & Parks, 2014; Dori-Hacohen & Shavit, 2013); as well as academic lectures, guided tours, roasts, and so on. From an EC perspective, when determining what the genre of a given speech event is, it's important to take into account the genre that the participants ascribe it to.

Why Speech Events Matter

Some speech events are special or unusual activities that people participate in only infrequently, such as marriage ceremonies (Leeds-Hurwitz, 2002) or jury deliberation (Sprain & Gastil, 2013). Some speech events turn into social dramas, stirring controversy and disagreement (Philipsen, 1986; Turner, 1980); many, though, are routine everyday activities like business meetings (Molina-Markham, 2014) or social/cultural exchanges (Kvam, 2017). Regardless of whether they are mundane or remarkable, contentious or peaceable, speech events remain one of the most important units of analysis for EC scholars (Hymes, 1974; Saville-Troike, 2003). Their great variety makes them endlessly appealing as a focus of study, and their potential for revealing rich information about a group's culture is high (Hymes, 1962).

For example, you can study a speech event to learn about a community's members and the relationships between them. This, by extension, can reveal much about how the community functions, including its norms, rules, and premises. This is exemplified in a particular study of a ritualized public speaking event called "speaking for others," which occurs among the Osage people, a Native American community (Pratt & Wieder, 1993). With this speech event, the featured speakers are male elders who have spent time attending to and learning the traditions and "Osage ways" from other members. A close analysis of this event provides rich insights on how gender, age, knowledge, and history shape the organization of this community (Pratt & Wieder, 1993).

Similarly, studying speech events can help newcomers "learn about the sociocultural life" (Sprain & Boromisza-Habashi, 2012, p. 185) of a different cultural group. For example, one EC scholar spent an extended period of time in Germany, where she was introduced to a speech event called *Bruderschaft trinken*, loosely translated from the German language as "drinking to brotherhood" (Winchatz, 1999). With this speech event, which usually happens when people are drinking and celebrating together, people proclaim that they are changing their relationship from mere acquaintances to something more intimate, like friendship. They "offer the *du*" to one another, which means that they invite each other to stop using the formal German personal pronoun *Sie* in favor of the informal *du* (Winchatz, 1999, 2001). Finally, they lift their glasses and toast this new standing in their relationships. Although it may seem inconsequential, the *Bruderschaft trinken* speech act marks what will be a significant shift in how the participants will talk to and interact with one another from this moment on.

As all of these examples show, studying speech events is a very useful way to learn about a group's culture, including how to demonstrate communicative competence (Hymes, 1972b; Witteborn, 2003). This is certainly helpful for people who are navigating a new community and/or a new cultural locale. Even beyond that, though, using the ethnography of communication to study speech events can help us practice the challenging task of unpacking and understanding other people's ways from *their* perspectives, while simultaneously withholding our own personal judgments on those ways (Philipsen, 1989–1990, 2010b). This does not mean that we can never evaluate what we observe in the field; on the contrary, EC research can be the basis for identifying social problems and working toward social justice (Scollon & Wong Scollon, 2009). However, studying speech events and other communicative phenomena with EC tools requires that we develop an empathetic understanding of people's lived realities as our first order of business.

Studying Speech Events in the Field

- What kinds of speech events have you have participated in or observed within your new cultural environment?
- Are there any unique types of speech events that happen in your new cultural environment that you haven't observed anywhere else?
- What kinds of speech events seem especially important, significant, and/or meaningful to this cultural community?
- Which speech events in your new community interest you the most? Why?

Jot down your ideas, thoughts, and interests below.

```
_____

_____

_____

_____

_____
```

Look back at your ideas. For practical purposes, it will be very helpful if you examine a speech event that is organized, scheduled, frequent, or accessible enough that you can be sure of observing it.

With this in mind, select one speech event that you'd like to examine at your field site and write it in the box below.

The speech event that I will study is ...
I can be reasonably sure of observing and collecting data on this speech event because ...

Ethics: Confidentiality

In contrast to privacy and anonymity (covered in Chapter 5), which is about protecting the people whom you study, the concept of **confidentiality** pertains to safeguarding the actual data that you collect. Specifically, when social scientists talk about confidentiality in research, they are referring to how data (jottings, field notes, recordings, photographs, textual materials, etc.) are handled by the researcher—which is you, in this case. Whenever you collect data for any type of research project, you are responsible for protecting it on behalf of the people who have shared it with you. This means not only keeping it private but also protecting it from improperly being seen by anyone other than you and safely disposing of it when it is no longer needed.

Write in your answers to the questions below. Be prepared to explain your answers to your own participants, ideally before you collect your data, thus giving them the opportunity to decline participation if they so desire.

1. How/where will you store each type of data that you collect (paper, electronic, audio/video recordings, photographs, etc.)?

_____

_____

_____

_____

_____

_____

_____

_____

_____

_____

_____

2. How will you ensure the security of your stored data?

_____

_____

_____

_____

_____

_____

_____

_____

_____

_____

_____

3. Will anyone besides you have access to these data? If so, who and why? How exactly will they access it?

_____

4. Will you permanently delete the data that you collect after your project is done? If yes, when and how? If not, why not?

_____

Fieldwork: Combining Methods In Situ

As with all the aspects of communication covered in this workbook, it is important to look at speech events **in situ**; that is, situated in the places where they occur (Hymes, 1964). For an ethnographer, to be *in situ* means to be wherever the interaction is taking place, whether online or offline, in person or by using some kind of technological platform, and so on. By being in situ you will be able to collect primary, firsthand data on actual speech events, which is the best kind of data from an ethnographic perspective (Silverman, 2005).

To collect your data while in situ, you should organize your own direct observations or participant observations for your chosen speech event. While engaging in your observations, document the speech event in as much detail as possible, whether by making detailed jottings (Chapter 2) and then using them to write up field notes (Chapter 6), collecting video or audio recordings and transcribing them (Chapter 5), conducting interviews (Chapter 4), collecting relevant texts (Chapter 3), or any combination of these.

Data Analysis

After collecting your data (jottings, field notes, interviews, transcripts, textual materials, etc.), use the SPEAKING framework to organize and analyze all of the materials in your data set. Aim for as detailed a description as possible for each component of the SPEAKING framework. Write up your descriptions below.

Setting, scene	

Participants	
Ends	
Act sequence	

Key	
Instrumentalities	
Norms	
Genre	

Write a Research Memo

Now, in the space below, write up a research memo on what you noticed and learned about the speech event that you studied. What might your observations suggest or reveal about cultural life there?

_____

_____

_____

_____

_____

_____

_____

_____

_____

_____

_____

_____

_____

Check Your Work

Do members of the cultural group that you are studying agree with your analysis? Share what you have observed with one or more people in the group to get their feedback. To what extent do they agree with your discoveries? Are there any points that they would adjust to make them more accurate? How?

_____

_____

_____

_____

_____

_____

_____

Reflections and Recommendations

Before moving on to the next chapter, take a moment to jot down some of your reflections, questions, ideas, and recommendations on the work that you just did, answering any of the following questions.

1. What were your main takeaways from doing this work?

2. Did you make any "bonus" discoveries that weren't necessarily related to the main concepts that you were studying? Ethnographers often end up with interesting data that isn't directly relevant to what they are focusing on. Rather than throwing those data away, make note of them here in case you'd like to follow up at a later time.

3. Did you have any difficulties or disappointing results when you did this work? If yes, don't worry; this is a natural part of doing ethnographic research and something that you can definitely learn from. Take a moment to reflect on any setbacks here. What were they, and why do you think they occurred? How might you avoid them if you were to do this work again?

4. What do's and don'ts would you pass on to your future self if you were to study the concepts covered in this chapter again? What would you do differently, and why?

5. What additional questions arose while you were doing this work? If you were going to continue with or expand this work, what would you want to explore? How might you deepen or expand your work?

6. What other placeholders, notes, or reminders would you like to set down for yourself here?

_____

_____

_____

_____

_____

_____

_____

_____

_____

_____

_____

_____

_____

_____

_____

Optional Deep Dive

▶ For more on the SPEAKING heuristic, see Trudy Milburn's online module on The Ethnography of Communication, an entry in the Electronic Encyclopedia of Communication published by the Communication Institute for Online Scholarship (CIOS) at https://tinyurl.com/yyv4qpje

▶ For an ethnographer's take on data security, see the online article "Encrypting Ethnography: Digital Security for Researchers," written by Jonatan Kurzwelly and published on the Savage Minds anthropology research blog at https://tinyurl.com/y7pawypt

▶ See also Alexander Taylor's article, "Cloud Security for Anthropologists," on the anthro{-dendum} blog at https://tinyurl.com/yy5bb6e8

Speech Codes

Throughout this book you have learned how to use the EC approach to study different aspects of cultural communication, including speech acts (Chapter 2); symbolic terms (Chapter 3); metacommunication (Chapter 4); cognitive scripts (Chapter 5); norms, rules, and premises (Chapter 6); and speech events (Chapter 7). Now, in this final chapter, we will tie all of these together with a unifying concept (speech codes) and a theory (speech codes theory) that, taken together, provide an overarching framework for navigating new cultural environments.

Definition of a Speech Code

As this book has been describing, the ethnography of communication approach follows the ethnographic tradition in its use of sustained immersion in a field site, during which the ethnographer observes and participates in the routine activities of the group. This kind of participant observation allows the ethnographer to collect a richly descriptive ethnographic data set on people's lived experiences. The data set is usually composed of a lot of jottings and field notes, as well as interviews, videos, photos, transcripts of talk and/or interactions, and other textual materials. Once the data have been collected, ethnographers of communication look specifically at people's communication practices, combing the data set for evidence of speech acts; symbolic terms; metacommunication; cognitive scripts; norms, rules, and premises; and speech events.

It is at this point that speech codes theorists take the analysis one step further to discern an overarching **speech code** that shapes the unique cultural life of the group. A *speech code* is defined as "a system of socially constructed symbols and meanings, premises, and rules, pertaining to communicative conduct" (Philipsen, 1997, p. 126). As noted elsewhere in this book, ethnographers of communication use the term "speech" as shorthand for all types of communication, not just verbal but also nonverbal, gestural, technology mediated, text based, and other symbolic forms of interaction between people, even silence (Carbaugh, 2005; Covarrubias, 2009; Hart, 2017b; Philipsen et al., 2005; Saville-Troike, 2003). For this reason, when we talk about *speech codes*, we are actually talking about codes pertaining to all types of human communication. As *systems*, speech codes are configurations of interconnected symbols, norms, rules, premises, and so on. That is, a speech code is not a random rule, just one premise, or an arbitrary symbol. Instead, it is a set of symbols, norms, rules, premises, and so on, all of which work together to express and instantiate a group's culture.

One recent example of a speech code comes from research that I conducted on Eloqi, a pseudonym for a private language teaching community that existed online for about 5 years in the early 2000s (Hart, 2015, 2016). Eloqi employed language trainers who were based in the United States to teach English lessons to students based in China. All of the lessons taught by Eloqi's trainers took place on the company's proprietary online platform, through which the trainers and students communicated with each other using text and voice.

One of Eloqi's founders was a friend of mine, whose chats with me about his new start-up piqued my curiosity. Interested in learning about Eloqi's organizational culture, I asked my friend for permission to do this research, which he and the other company leaders granted. I then went through the process of getting my research approved by my university's Human Subjects Division. This required me to write up a detailed plan about how exactly I would collect and analyze all of my data. Most importantly, my plan had to include the exact communication that I would use to ask for each participant's informed consent. Once my study had been approved, I was able to start collecting my data.

It took me the better part of a year to collect my data, during which time I worked as an Eloqi trainer. As an Eloqi trainer, I went about my regular business in the online community, engaging with my colleagues, attending team meetings, and of course teaching the company's online English lessons. Simultaneously, I was also doing the work of an ethnographer of communication, which required me to pay close attention to everything that I was observing and experiencing at my virtual field site. Whenever I spoke with people directly, I had to first ask for their informed consent, both to let me ask questions and to record our interactions. I had to properly store each piece of data that I collected, maintaining people's privacy as well as the confidentiality of what they had shared with me. I then had to analyze the data, looking for patterns and trying to interpret what it all meant. And finally, I wrote up a research report (my doctoral dissertation) to share my findings with other people.

To complete this entire project, I used every method of data collection described in this book. I spent the better part of a year doing the participant observations at my virtual field site, creating jottings and then transforming them into field notes. I collected recordings of naturally occurring talk like team meetings and online lessons, which I then transcribed. I gathered textual artifacts like screenshots, materials from the company website, training materials, and meeting minutes. Lastly, I conducted a series of interviews with Eloqi administrators, trainers, and students, some in person and some online, which I recorded and transcribed.

Once I had finished the data collection, I had amassed hundreds of pages of electronic data. I anonymized everything and stored it on a password-protected laptop, which I also used for my data analysis. Because I had so much material, it helped me to use software for the data analysis; the program I chose was TAMS Analyzer (Weinstein, 2008). Like any other type of qualitative data analysis software, the program that I chose was designed to assist researchers with storing, coding, and sorting through data; while it doesn't do the work for you, it certainly makes it easier (Hart & Achterman, 2017). To analyze the data, I began by scrutinizing the entire data set, bit by bit, looking for evidence of symbolic terms; speech acts; metacommunication; cognitive scripts; and norms, rules, and premises. Consistent with the guidelines presented in this book, I was looking for recurring patterns in the data, rather than one-offs or isolated events. It took months of work, but in the end I did identify a speech code that was operating in the Eloqi community, which I named *the code of English logic* (Hart, 2016).

The code of English logic, as it functioned at Eloqi, consisted of one symbolic term, *native English*, and six rules that guided Eloqi community members on how to produce their idea of native English speech in a competent way. The rules were that

- speech should be organized
- speakers should be succinct and not ramble
- speakers should produce spontaneous rather than "canned" speech
- speakers should be original and honest in their communication
- speakers should take the initiative and be proactive in their communication
- speakers should be positive and supportive of one another (Hart, 2016)

Taken holistically, the members of the Eloqi community used this speech code—the code of English logic—to establish, evaluate, and maintain what counted as good and appropriate communication. The code of English logic also reflected some of the Eloqi community's values, such as honesty, initiative, and being supportive of one another. And, while the code of English logic does not give us a complete picture of Eloqi's culture, it does reveal some significant aspects of it, which were important for any newcomers who wanted to be successful within the group.

Explanation of Speech Codes Theory

A **theory** is an "organized set of concepts, explanations, and principles that depicts some aspect of human experience. Theories are formulated in order to help explain and understand phenomena ... [and] develop knowledge" (Littlejohn et al., 2016, p. 7). Theories are "held together" by **propositions**, which are "relational statements about how [that theory's] concepts are related to each other" (McGregor, 2018, pp.

76–77). Broadly, **speech codes theory** was developed to explain, understand, and generate knowledge on the relationship between culture and communication. It has six propositions, all of which are based on previous social scientific research. Like any good theoretical proposition, SCT's propositions are testable; furthermore, they have all been tested through subsequent research. Here is a short overview of the six propositions of SCT, as articulated in Philipsen et al. (2005).

SCT Proposition #1: A Distinctive Culture

"Wherever there is a distinctive culture, there is to be found a distinctive speech code."

(Philipsen et al., 2005, p. 58)

A foundational assumption of speech codes theory is that *culture* can be understood as a *code* of communicative conduct; that is, a configuration of interconnected symbols, rules, premises, norms, and so on pertaining to communication practices. Going along with this, Proposition #1 of speech codes theory recognizes that each cultural group has its own unique speech code. Whether one group's speech code is very similar to or radically different from another's, the important thing is that speech codes are distinctive to the group.

For example, the Teamsterville speech code of honor was documented in a White working-class neighborhood in Chicago, Illinois, in the late 1960s and early 1970s (Philipsen, 1975, 1986, 1992). This particular code was based on the concept of social hierarchy, which exerted a strong influence on the community's value system (Philipsen, 1992). A speech code theorist would suggest that, while other communities might have similar speech codes to that of the Teamstervillers, no other group's code would be exactly the same. Rather, all speech codes are distinctive in their own way.

SCT Proposition #2: Multiple Speech Codes

"In any given speech community, multiple speech codes are deployed."

(Philipsen et al., 2005, p. 59)

From an SCT perspective, a community is a group of people who "claim [some] commonalit[ies] derived from shared identity" (Philipsen, 1987, p. 249). That identity may be grounded in a shared organization, profession, age, gender, region, nationality, or any combination of these or other aspects. With this in mind, this proposition states that multiple and sometimes even contrasting or competing speech codes can coexist within the same community. For example, research done on how the U.S. government explained and justified its decisions during the Vietnam War revealed two conflicting speech codes at work in U.S. society—the *speech code of rationality* and the opposing *speech code of spirituality* (Coutu, 2000). The code of rationality placed great value on debate and open discussion as prerequisites for good decision making. The code of spirituality, on the other hand, emphasized faith and morality, and it relied on decency and virtue for making good decisions. In the case of the U.S. government's decision making in the time of the Vietnam War, the administration was operating by the code of rationality, whereas the public at large was applying the code of spirituality. To a large extent, the discord between the government and the public was due to differing speech codes. In fact, many studies that apply the ethnography of communication and/or speech codes theory demonstrate that conflict can arise when different speech codes are at stake (Carbaugh, 2005; Coutu, 2008; Covarrubias, 2002).

SCT Proposition #3: Distinctive Psychology, Sociology, and Rhetoric

"A speech code implicates a culturally distinctive psychology, sociology, and rhetoric."

(Philipsen et al., 2005, p. 61)

This proposition is directly linked to a theme present throughout this book; namely, that communication reveals a great deal about culture. Here, "*psychology* [in the context of speech codes theory] refers to ideas about personhood, including notions about what a 'proper' person is, and how such persons should conduct themselves" (Hart, 2017b, p. 4). "Sociology" means how "people define their group and/or other groups, and ... how people should interact with or relate to others within the group, and/or those outside of it" (Hart, 2017b, p. 4). "Rhetoric" relates to group members' beliefs about how to strategically use communication "to achieve the desired ends" (Hart, 2017b, p. 4). In other words, a speech code embodies a community's beliefs about how to be a good person, how to properly interact with other people, and how to communicate with others.

This proposition is illustrated by work on the code of English logic (Hart, 2016), which revealed the Eloqi community's emphasis on being an open and honest person with a positive attitude and being proactive in the world (psychology). Eloqi community members were expected to be positive, supportive, and honest toward others in their group (sociology). Finally, Eloqi members were concerned with speaking in a way that was deemed succinct, organized, and spontaneous (rhetoric). In sum, as the Eloqi case demonstrates, a speech code reveals a local blueprint for being a competent member of a cultural group (Hart, 2017b). Therefore, by analyzing a group's speech code(s), we can learn a lot about their beliefs, values, and way of life; that is, their culture.

SCT Proposition #4: The (Local) Significance of Speaking

> "The significance of speaking is contingent upon the speech codes used by interlocutors to constitute the meanings of communicative acts."
>
> (Philipsen et al., 2005, p. 62)

According to this proposition, "the ways in which a person hears, interprets, understands, and/or acts upon communication are shaped by the speech codes under which they operate" (Hart, 2017b, p. 5). For example, in Teamsterville, if boys were misbehaving, it was thought that the man in charge should stop the misbehavior by physically disciplining those boys; that is, by hitting them. For community members who were operating under the code of honor, this was seen as the proper response and was therefore interpreted in a positive manner. If the man in charge went against the code of honor, perhaps by trying to turn the other cheek or by attempting to talk with the boys, the other Teamstervillers would "hear" this communication as unacceptably weak or even deviant (Philipsen, 1975, 1986, 1992). In other words, a community's speech code is the measuring stick by which members interpret and evaluate communication.

SCT Proposition #5: The Codes Woven Into Local Communication

> "The terms, rules, and premises of a speech code are inextricably woven into speaking itself."
>
> (Philipsen et al., 2005, p. 62)

If you are wondering how to find a community's speech codes, this proposition of speech codes theory provides the answer: we find speech codes by looking at community members' regular, day-to-day communication practices. In other words, we should study the group's communication, including their speech acts; symbolic terms; metacommunication; cognitive scripts; norms, rules, and premises; and speech events, just as described throughout this book. Any form of communication can legitimately be studied, whether face-to-face, technology mediated, text based, gestural, and so on. We can study communication practices over long stretches of time or in finite instances, like a conversation or a public speech. Whatever the case, we must look at real, situated communication practices to find speech codes.

SCT Proposition #6: Predicting and Explaining Communicative Conduct

"The artful use of a shared speech code is a sufficient condition for predicting, explaining, and controlling the form of discourse about the intelligibility, prudence, and morality of communicative conduct."

(Philipsen et al., 2005, p. 63)

The final proposition of speech codes theory relates back to the general function of theory, which, as noted earlier, is to help us understand, explain, and predict things happening in the world. When Proposition #6 of speech codes theory talks about people's "artful use" of speech codes, it means that when community members use their group's speech code and use it well, they can probably anticipate the effect that it will have on their fellow community members. For example, when a Teamsterville man in charge of a group of misbehaving boys dealt with the situation by hitting those boys, he knew that other group members would likely approve and would view him as competent. Another example of this can be seen among the Eloqi members who used the code of English logic. They believed that "good" English speech should be succinct and positive. If a member of this community told a long, rambling story rather than getting quickly to the point, they could expect to be corrected, but when they got right to the point, they were praised. Likewise, if they expressed negative feelings about themselves, they were likely to be asked to change their attitude, and their original message might be ignored.

Importantly, though, a caveat to Proposition #6 and to speech codes theory in general is that while speech codes are indeed very influential, they do not predetermine communication (Philipsen et al., 2005). That is, people are not robotically controlled by speech codes imprinted into their brains. On the contrary, people can and do challenge speech codes all the time. Furthermore, speech codes are not set in stone for all eternity; rather, just as cultures shift and change over time, so too do speech codes (Philipsen et al., 2005).

Why Speech Codes Matter

The ethnography of communication and speech codes theory are premised on the belief that studying a group's communication is an effective way to understand that group's culture. Put differently, with the right training (which this book is intended to provide), you can analyze culture from the inside out by immersing yourself within a cultural environment, paying close attention to that group's communication practices, and unpacking the local significance of those practices. By extension, speech codes matter because they reveal, express, shape, and reify a group's culture; so by studying speech codes, you can come to understand the culture of the group or community that uses those codes (Boromisza-Habashi, 2017; Philipsen, 2003).

If you understand a local speech code, this opens up new and fruitful possibilities. For example, if you are a new member of a group, studying speech codes can give you a practical advantage as you navigate that setting and learn about the local ways of doing things there. Understanding local speech codes can help you interpret communicative activity in your community and make strategic choices about your own communicative behavior. If you know the local codes, you might be able to make predictions about the group's communicative actions and anticipate the results that those actions are likely to have. And, when there is conflict within the group or between groups, analyzing the local speech codes can be a way to understand and perhaps even to resolve that conflict.

Finding a Speech Code in Your Data

Every chapter in this book has helped you identify different aspects of communication at your cultural site. Now, in the final chapter of this book, you will look at all of your data holistically, reflecting on what all these pieces together reveal about a speech code or codes. To this end, go back and review all of the data that you collected from each chapter. Look for patterns in the data; that is, things that seem to repeat regularly.

Chapter 2.   What kinds of speech acts did you examine, and what did those speech acts reveal about the community?

Chapter 3.   What symbolic terms did you find, and what did they reveal about the community?

Chapter 4.   What kind of metacommunication did you examine, and what did that reveal about the community?

Chapter 5.   What cognitive script did you look at, and what did it illustrate about the community?

Chapter 6.   What norms, rules, and premises did you find, and what did they illustrate about the community?

Chapter 7.   What speech event did you examine? What did you learn? What did it reveal about the community?

As you pull all your findings from Chapters 2–7 together, what patterns or themes do you notice across the data set?

_____

_____

_____

_____

_____

_____

_____

Now try looking for traces of a speech code in those patterns. Recall that a speech code is an interconnected *system* of "symbols and meanings, premises, and rules, pertaining to communicative conduct" (Philipsen, 1997, p. 126). In other words, a speech code is not a random rule here and there or just one premise or symbol. Instead, to find a speech code—or traces of one—we are looking for repeated patterns of symbols, meaning, norms, rules, premises, and so on. Seeing a pattern means that you'll see themes occurring and reoccurring again and again in your data set. To look for a speech code, use the theory's propositions and their inherent questions as a guide.

Applying SCT Proposition #2

"In any given speech community, multiple speech codes are deployed."

Did you find traces of multiple speech codes? If yes, are they conflicting? Explain your answers below.

_____

_____

_____

_____

_____

_____

_____

_____

_____

_____

_____

Applying SCT Proposition #3

"A speech code implicates a culturally distinctive psychology, sociology, and rhetoric."

Looking at your data, what examples or excerpts can you find about the following points? What patterns can you detect?

- *Psychology:* What is the "right" kind of person in the community that you studied? What is the proper way to be? Conversely, what are some examples of being the "wrong" kind of person in this community?

- *Sociology:* What are the "boundaries" of the group; that is, who counts as a member and who does not? How do members define or characterize their group or community? What do they stand for? How do members believe they ought to interact with or relate to other members? How do they believe they ought to interact with or relate to people outside of their group?

- *Rhetoric:* How do community members use communication to get things done in the world? What is the "right" way to communicate? Conversely, what do members feel is the "wrong" way to communicate?

_____
_____
_____
_____
_____
_____
_____
_____
_____
_____

Applying SCT Proposition #4

"The significance of speaking is contingent upon the speech codes used by inter-
locutors to constitute the meanings of communicative acts."

Looking across your data, what examples can you find of how people in the community
use their speech code or codes to "hear," interpret, and/or evaluate communication?

_____
_____
_____
_____
_____
_____
_____
_____
_____
_____
_____
_____

Applying SCT Proposition #5

"The terms, rules, and premises of a speech code are inextricably woven into speaking itself."

Looking across your data, what traces of a speech code or codes can you discover in people's communication? What excerpts can you point to where the code is suggested or articulated, whether explicitly or implicitly?

_____
_____
_____
_____
_____
_____
_____
_____
_____
_____

Applying SCT Proposition #6

"The artful use of a shared speech code is a sufficient condition for predicting, explaining, and controlling the form of discourse about the intelligibility, prudence, and morality of communicative conduct."

Looking across your data, can you find examples or instances in which knowing the local speech code or codes could help you anticipate how certain communication activities or practices would play out and/or how people would be likely to respond? Describe those below.

_____

_____

_____

_____

_____

_____

_____

_____

_____

_____

_____

Applying SCT Proposition #1

Finally, we come back to proposition #1 of speech codes theory, which states that,

"wherever there is a distinctive culture, there is to be found a distinctive speech code."

What traces of a speech code did you find in your data? How do those traces of a speech code or codes illuminate something distinctive or unique about the community that you studied? About their culture?

_____

_____

_____

_____

_____

_____

_____

_____

_____

_____

_____

Name Your Speech Code(s)

Perhaps you saw only faint traces of a speech code in your data, or maybe you've discovered resoundingly strong evidence of a code or even multiple codes. Maybe you've even found evidence of conflicting codes. Whatever the case may be, take the next (fun) step of choosing a name for the speech code or codes that you found.

I'm naming the speech code(s) that I found:
the code of   *the code of*   *the code of*

For future reference, whenever you find a speech code, it is a good idea to research whether the code that you found is similar or related to any speech codes reported on by other ethnographers of communication.

Ethics: Making Generalizations vs. Stereotyping

An important addendum to the work that we are doing here, and indeed to any social scientific analysis of culture or intercultural communication, is that while we may be able to draw generalizations from our research, we must avoid any type of stereotyping.

To clarify, **generalizations** "are statements about the characteristics and behaviors that describe a percentage of the members of a cultural group" (Kurylo, 2013, p. 6). Importantly, generalizations are based on research and can be tested and verified (Kurylo, 2013). For example, a generalization about people who identify as culturally Japanese is that, on average, they report feeling more comfortable with longer silences in conversation than Americans do (Morrison, 2017). One study on this topic found that the average Japanese respondent felt comfortable with up to 8.2 seconds of silence, while the average American felt comfortable with only half that amount of silence (Morrison, 2017). This generalization isn't set in stone, of course; over time, people's habits, preferences, and beliefs can and do shift. For this reason, generalizations should be periodically retested and updated, since they are subject to change.

Stereotypes, on the other hand, are blanket assumptions about groups and all of their members (Kurylo, 2013). Stereotypes can be framed neutrally, positively, or negatively; thinking, for example, that all Italian people are excellent cooks is just as much a stereotype as saying that all English people are bad ones. Going back to our original example, it's a stereotype to assume that just because a person identifies as Japanese, they will definitely or automatically feel comfortable with long stretches of silence in a conversation. As you have learned firsthand from doing the ethnographic work that this book has guided you through, it's simply not true that every single member of a community thinks, feels, and acts the same way in the same context across all time. Herein lies a major problem with using stereotypes—they are not only the product of sloppy thinking, they are also inherently false. Unfortunately, stereotypes are prone to getting fossilized or stuck in our social and personal narratives; many are mistakenly treated as enduring truths. This is another reason why doing rigorous EC work is so important, because it can help us generate nuanced understandings of local communities and cultures and counteract harmful stereotypes.

When using the EC/SCT framework to study communication in local communities, the hope is that we will be able to identify some patterns or truths that hold across the group *in general*. As argued in this book, finding those patterns can help us better understand communities and their cultures, which can help us be more competent members of those groups. When we develop and make use of generalizations, we are obliged to acknowledge that, despite their utility, they always have limitations. No study of a cultural community can ever be complete or exhaustive. As social scientists, we develop generalizations from our findings only when we have sufficient evidence to do so. When we express them, we are careful to explain how we developed them and what communities and contexts we derived them from. This is how we stay honest about and accountable for the limitations of what we learn.

Ethics: Promoting Change and Pushing for Justice

Ethnographers of communication are expected to engage in their research "with an attitude of exploration … [and] with curiosity about what may be found [at their field sites]" (Philipsen, 2010a, p. 87). An important aspect of this exploratory and curious attitude is that EC researchers should hold back on judging or evaluating the people, communities, and cultures that they are examining (Philipsen, 1989–1990). It's not that ethnographers believe that they can be totally objective or neutral in their research—they don't. In keeping with the interpretive tradition in which their scholarship is grounded, EC researchers acknowledge that bias and judgment can creep into their work in many different ways, from choosing a community to focus on, to selecting what to observe and what to leave out, to deciding whom to interview, and even right down to how they transcribe their data. Nevertheless, one of the main commitments that ethnographers of communication make when they embark on their work is to document, understand, and report on how their participants experience the world *on their own terms and in their own words.* EC scholars must do this in a way that is "accurate, careful, and sensitive" (Philipsen, 1989–1990, p. 260) so that they can properly articulate participants' truths to the rest of the world. As you have learned throughout this book, this makes the whole EC approach a powerful way to understand local communities *from the inside out.* We go in with an open mind, we walk around in community members' shoes, we explore the world from their vantage points, and then we write up ethnographic reports so that others may share in these understandings.

This leads to our final set of discussion questions about conducting ethnographic work, which addresses the issue of change. Does doing ethnographic research mean that we have to limit ourselves to looking and learning, or can we get involved in the communities that we study? Can we promote any type of change with our EC/SCT research, whether practical or social? Can we advocate for social justice?

First, it's important to recognize that, regardless of an ethnographer's intentions, change is simply inevitable. Speech codes theory itself acknowledges that speech codes—like communication and culture in general—are never fixed or frozen. Rather, they arise out of and continually change through the "historically situated, ongoing communicative process[es] in which participants in the life of a social world construct, express, and negotiate the terms on which they conduct their lives together" (Philipsen, 2003, p. 53). In other words, like it or not, change is always happening, whether incrementally or drastically, as an inevitable part of the human experience.

But what, for example, should you do with the findings that you generate from your EC/SCT research? What if you believe that what you learned has practical applications beyond you being able to better navigate your field site? What if you learned things that you think community members could actually use to make their lives better? In fact, EC work was originally conceived as a way to contribute to the improvement of "the human condition" (Saville-Troike, 2003, p. 252; cf. Blommaert, 2009). In keeping with this tradition, recent scholarship has embraced and promoted the applied value of EC/SCT work, demonstrating that it has great potential to bring about positive, practical change (Sprain & Boromisza-Habashi, 2013), including in areas as varied as the design of strategic plans (Witteborn et al., 2013); pedagogy (Leighter et al., 2013; Townsend, 2013); health interventions (Ho, 2006; Witteborn et al., 2013); usability studies and user experience research (Carbaugh et al., 2013; Hart, 2015; Milburn, 2015a); and even peace building (Leighter et al., 2013; Miller & Rudnick, 2012).

And what if you desire more than practical change? What if you want to critique or push back against a local speech code? What if you feel that disruption rather than adaptation is warranted? Interestingly, the original EC scholars strongly envisioned this approach as an inherently democratic "science 'of the people'" (Blommaert, 2009, p. 258). They hoped that many citizen ethnographers would use it in their own communities, as part of their quests for equality and social justice (Blommaert, 2009). These original scholars firmly believed in the value of EC for "allowing different voices to speak … [and] constantly call[ing] into question the status of 'truth'" (Blommaert, 2009, p. 258). By using EC to analyze communication, community, and culture, they felt that we could make visible "the workings of powers and the deep structures of inequality in society" (Blommaert, 2009, p. 265). By bringing inequality to the light of day, they believed that we would ultimately be able to fight against it.

By deeply and richly understanding a local community, an ethnographer of communication can be poised to inspire, advocate, or fight for change. With that in mind, what are your thoughts on the questions below?

1. What might be your reasons for wanting to better understand a community that you are a member of?

2. If you are interested in promoting change, what kind of change would that be and why?

3. What would you like to do with the knowledge that you have gained, or could gain, through doing EC research? How could you put that knowledge to use?

Join the SCT Conversation

Gerry Philipsen, the originator of speech codes theory (1992, 1997), always intended for the theory to be open to revision and improvement; accordingly, it has been revised in response to feedback (Philipsen et al., 2005) and used by many scholars around the world, many of whom are cited in this book.

Now that you have learned how to use speech codes theory to conduct your own research on cultural communication, you are invited to join in on the scholarly conversation.

- Based on the work that you did using this book, how would you say speech codes theory performed?

- Having tried and tested the theory, do you have any ideas about how the theory could or should be modified? Is there anything you would change about it?

- Do you have any suggestions about how speech codes theory could be improved?

Write down your thoughts below, and if you feel inspired, share them with me at sct@tabithahart.net.

Closing Thoughts

Like most other scientific projects, the ethnography of communication is at once an intellectual and a highly practical endeavor. It is also fueled by an abiding faith in humanity, hope for progress and equality, and commitment to being part of the change. Ethnographers of communication use their specialized training to explore, analyze, and generate new knowledge and insights about different cultural groups. They use their findings to pose questions, engage others in dialogue, suggest new ways of doing things, and design strategic actions. Many of them use their work as a way to stretch toward the better world that they see within our reach. In completing a crash course on the ethnography of communication, you have joined the ranks of a long and impressive line of scholars, and you have embarked upon a worthy endeavor. There is much good work still to be done. Where will you go from here?

Optional Deep Dive

How ethnographers represent or give voice to the people that they study is a complex, contested, and weighty issue, one that merits careful consideration. It is a topic that has been meaningfully debated and addressed by critical ethnographers in particular.

▶ To learn more, see the (Critical) Ethnography Guidelines on the Teaching English to Speakers of Other Languages (TESOL) International Association website at https://tinyurl. com/yyrjod9r

Glossary

Anonymity: When used in reference to data collection, it means that the researcher collects information about unknown (anonymous) participants.

Cognitive script: A mental model that tells a person how to properly engage in different types of activities in particular environments.

Communication: A catch-all term for any type of social interaction, from face-to-face and verbal speech to nonverbal, text-based, technology-mediated communication and more.

Community: A group of people who share a feeling of commonality with one another, whether that feeling is based on their common interests, identities, affiliations, professions, roles, jobs, language(s), traditions, responsibilities, goals, or any other factor.

Confidentiality: When used in reference to data collection, it means safeguarding the actual data that you collect, including keeping it private, protecting it from improperly being seen or used, and safely disposing of it when it is no longer needed.

Culture: For EC/SCT scholars, culture isn't equated with a country, identity, or nationality. Instead, it is seen as communication and, more specifically, as a speech code; that is, a set of beliefs about communicative conduct, including (but not limited to) the symbols, norms, rules, premises, and values that people use to guide their communication.

Data: As used in this book, data is all the information that you collect while doing EC/SCT research. This can include notes and field notes, jottings, textual artifacts, recordings, transcriptions, and more.

Data analysis: In research, the process of sorting through and scrutinizing data and making sense of it.

Ethics: In research, the moral principles used to guide the processes of planning, conducting, and reporting on research.

Ethnography of communication: A theoretical/methodological framework for studying culture and communication from the inside out.

Field notes: Highly detailed written accounts of observations made in the field.

Field site: A site or location where an EC/SCT scholar goes to observe people living their lives.

Fieldwork: The process of collecting data in real-life settings (field sites), to see and hear people's actual, day-to-day communication.

Findings: The discoveries that a researcher makes from collecting and analyzing data.

Generalizations: General statements based on research, made about the characteristics and behaviors of the members of a group. Can be tested and verified.

Goals: Aims or desires that people have in mind as they engage in communication. Implicit or "translucent" goals may be unspoken and not explicitly expressed.

In situ: To be situated in the places where social life and interactions are happening.

Informed consent: When participants give their informed consent, they agree to be part of your research, knowing all the risks and benefits that this could result in. To secure informed consent, researchers tell (i.e., inform) participants about the data that they would like to collect, how they would like to collect it, and whatever risks participation might impose.

Jottings: Simple notes that you write down while in the field to help you remember what you saw and heard.

Member checks: To conduct member checks means to solicit feedback from the people that you are studying.

Metacommunicative moments: Occasions on which people communicate about their own communication or the communication of other people, including what communication activities are (or are not) occurring, what those communicative activities mean, the value of those activities, and the morality or immorality of them.

Metacommunicative terms: Words or expressions about communication.

Norms: Informal "social rules" that tell us what we should and should not do in a given context.

Observations: In ethnographic research, observation means to go to a field site and watch what people are doing there.

Outcomes: What actually happens, as opposed to goals, which are what people desire or intend to happen.

Participant observations: In ethnographic research, participation observation means to go to a field site and participate in activities there while also watching what people are doing there.

Participants: The people whom EC/SCT researchers study at their field sites; also, the people involved in the communicative action in the field.

Premises: Communal beliefs and values that undergird people's communication.

Qualitative data analysis: A process of analyzing qualitative data, which are rich and descriptive data that cannot be reduced to numbers.

Research memos: Short, informally written accounts that the researcher creates at various stages in their project.

Rich points: Instances when a person feels sudden surprise or confusion, often suggesting the presence of a boundary between different cultures.

Rules: Expressions about what should or should not happen in particular settings under particular circumstances. Often written down, giving them a formal, official, or explicit status.

Setting or scene: The location where a communicative activity takes place.

SPEAKING heuristic: A tool for organizing and analyzing data on speech events. Each of the letters in its name (S-P-E-A-K-I-N-G) represents an aspect of a speech event that should be observed, described, and analyzed: setting/scene, participants, ends, act sequence, key, instrumentalities, norms, genre.

Speech act: A communicative activity that has a particular, practical function.

Speech code: A set of beliefs about communicative conduct, including the symbols, norms, rules, premises, and values that people use to guide their communication.

Speech codes theory: A theory developed to explain, understand, and generate knowledge on the relationship between culture and communication. It has six propositions.

Speech events: Communicative occasions or activities that can take many forms.

Stereotypes: Blanket assumptions about groups and all of their members.

Symbol: A sign, mark, gesture, action, image, person, and so on that represents or stands in for something else.

Symbolic term: A specific word or phrase that expresses a key concept or an idea that is significant to a cultural group.

Transcribe: To convert material into text.

Unit of analysis: In research, the thing that is being studied or analyzed.

Vulnerable: In research, to be vulnerable is to require extra care or support due to greater likelihood of being harmed—even unintentionally—by participating in research.

References

Agar, M. (1999). How to ask for a study in qualitatisch. *Qualitative Health Research*, *9*(5), 684–697.

Agar, M. (2006a). Culture: Can you take it anywhere? *International Journal of Qualitative Methods*, *5*(2).

Agar, M. (2006b). An ethnography by any other name. … *FQS: Forum Qualitative Social Research*, *7*(4).

Annenberg Media Center. (2016). Videotaping and recording in public in California: The basics. http://resources.uscannenbergmedia.com/2016/08/videotaping-and-recording-in-public-in-california-the-basics/

Antaki, C. (2017). *An introductory tutorial in conversation analysis*. Charles Antaki's online resources. http://ca-tutorials.lboro.ac.uk/intro1.htm

Associated Press. (2019, August 8). *Timeline of events in shooting of Michael Brown in Ferguson*. https://apnews.com/9aa32033692547699a3b61da8fd1fc62

Baetens, M. (2020, June 17). Customers are reportedly having tantrums over wearing masks. *The Detroit News*. https://www.detroitnews.com/story/entertainment/dining/2020/06/17/some-restaurant-bar-customers-arent-handling-mask-rules-well/3191705001/

Bailey, B. (1997). Communication of respect in interethnic service encounters. *Language in Society*, *26*(3), 327–356.

Bailey, B. (2016). Street remarks to women in five countries and four languages: Impositions of engagement and intimacy. *Sociolinguistic Studies*, *10*(4), 589–609.

Bailey, B. (2017a). Greetings and compliments or street harassment? Competing evaluations of street remarks in a recorded collection. *Discourse & Society*, *28*(4), 353–373.

Bailey, B. (2017b). Piropos [amorous flattery] as a cultural term for talk in the Spanish-speaking world. In D. Carbaugh (Ed.), *Handbook of communication in cross-cultural perspective* (pp. 195–207). Routledge.

Basso, K. H. (1979). *Portraits of "the Whiteman": Linguistic play and cultural symbols among the Western Apache*. Cambridge University Press.

Baxter, L. (1993). "Talking things through" and "putting it in writing": Two codes of communication in an academic institution. *Journal of Applied Communication Research, 21,* 313–326.

Blommaert, J. (2009). Ethnography and democracy: Hymes' political theory of language. *Text & Talk, 29*(3), 257–276.

Boromisza-Habashi, D. (2012). The cultural foundations of denials of hate speech in Hungarian broadcast talk. *Discourse & Communication, 6*(1), 3–20.

Boromisza-Habashi, D. (2013). *Speaking hatefully: Culture, communication, and political action in Hungary.* Pennsylvania State University Press.

Boromisza-Habashi, D. (2017). Cultural communication, overview. In Y. Y. Kim (Ed.), *The international encyclopedia of intercultural communication.* John Wiley & Sons.

Boromisza-Habashi, D., & Parks, R. M. (2014). The communal function of social interaction on an online academic newsgroup. *Western Journal of Communication, 78*(2), 194–212.

Boromisza-Habashi, D., & Reinig, L. (2018). Speech genres and cultural value in the Anglo-American public speaking course as a site of language socialization. *Journal of International and Intercultural Communication, 11*(2), 117–135.

Brule, N., & Eckstein, J. J. (2018). Vulnerable groups. In M. Allen (Ed.), *The SAGE encyclopedia of communication research methods,* 1871-1874. SAGE Publications.

Bunch, G. C. (2009). "Going up there": Challenges and opportunities for language minority students during a mainstream classroom speech event. *Linguistics and Education, 20,* 81–108.

Carbaugh, D. (1987). Communication rules in Donahue discourse. *Research on Language and Social Interaction, 21,* 31–61.

Carbaugh, D. (1989). Fifty terms for talk: A cross-cultural study. In S. Ting-Toomey & F. Korzenny (Eds.), *International and Intercultural Communication Annual* (Vol. 13, pp. 93–120). SAGE Publications.

Carbaugh, D. (1989–1990). The critical voice in ethnography of communication research. *Research on Language and Social Interaction, 23,* 261–282.

Carbaugh, D. (1995). The ethnographic communication theory of Philipsen and associates. In D. P. Cushman & B. Kovacic (Eds.), *Watershed research traditions in human communication theory* (pp. 269–297). State University of New York Press.

Carbaugh, D. (2005). *Cutures in conversation.* Lawrence Erlbaum Associates.

Carbaugh, D. (2007a). Cultural discourse analysis: Communication practices and intercultural encounters. *Journal of Intercultural Communication Research, 36*(3), 167–182.

Carbaugh, D., Berry, M., & Nurmikari-Berry, M. (2006). Coding personhood through cultural terms and practices: Silence and quietude as a Finnish "natural way of being." *Journal of Language and Social Psychology, 25*(3), 1–18.

Carbaugh, D., Lie, S., Locmele, L., & Sotirova, N. (2012). Ethnographic studies of intergroup communication. In H. Giles (Ed.), *The handbook of intergroup communication* (pp. 44–57). Routledge.

Carbaugh, D., Nuciforo, E. V., Saito, M., & Shin, D.-s. (2011). "Dialogue" in cross-cultural perspective: Japanese, Korean, and Russian discourses. *Journal of International and Intercultural Communication, 4*(2), 87–108.

Carbaugh, D., Winter, U., van Over, B., Molina-Markham, E., & Lie, S. (2013). Cultural analyses of in-car communication. *Journal of Applied Communication Research, 41*(2), 195–201.

Carbaugh, D. (2015). Ethnography of communication. In W. Donsbach (Ed.), *The international encyclopedia of communication*. John Wiley & Sons.

Carr, A. (2015, June 15). The inside story of Starbucks's Race Together campaign, no foam. *Fast Company*. https://www.fastcompany.com/3046890/the-inside-story-of-starbuckss-race-together-campaign-no-foam

Castor, T. (2009). "It's just a process": Questioning in the construction of a university crisis. *Discourse Studies, 11*(2), 179–197.

Centers for Disease Control and Prevention. (2020, July 17). *Considerations for restaurants and bars*. https://www.cdc.gov/coronavirus/2019-ncov/community/organizations/business-employers/bars-restaurants.html

Coutu, L. (2000). Communication codes of rationality and spirituality in the discourse of and about Robert S. McNamara's "In retrospect." *Research on Language and Social Interaction, 33*(2), 179–211.

Coutu, L. (2008). Contested social identity and communication in talk and text about the Vietnam War. *Research on Language and Social Interaction, 41*(4), 387–407.

Covarrubias, P. (2002). *Culture, communication, and cooperation: Interpersonal relations and pronominal address in a Mexican organization*. Rowman & Littlefield Publishers.

Covarrubias, P. (2009). Ethnography of communication. In S. W. Littlejohn & K. A. Foss (Eds.), *Encyclopedia of communication theory* (pp. 356-360). SAGE Publications.

Creswell, J. W. (2013). *Qualitative inquiry and research design: Choosing among five approaches* (3rd ed.). SAGE Publications.

Dainas, A. R., & Herring, S. C. (forthcoming). Interpreting emoji pragmatics. In C. Xie, F. Yus, & H. Haberland (Eds.), *Approaches to Internet pragmatics: Theory and practice*. John Benjamins Publishing Company.

Digital Medial Law Project. (2020). *Gathering private information*. http://www.dmlp.org/legal-guide/gathering-private-information

Dori-Hacohen, G., & Shavit, N. (2013). The cultural meanings of Israeli tokbek (talk-back online commenting) and their relevance to the online democratic public sphere. *International Journal of Electronic Governance, 6*(4), 361–379.

Edgerly, L. (2011). Difference and political legitimacy: Speakers' construction of "citizen" and "refugee" personae in talk about Hurricane Katrina. *Western Journal of Communication, 75*(3), 304–322.

Edgerly, L. (2017). Discourse of difference. In Y. Y. Kim (Ed.), *The international encyclopedia of intercultural communication.* John Wiley & Sons.

Electronic Code of Federal Regulations. (2018). *Part 46—protection of human subjects.* https://www.ecfr.gov/cgi-bin/retrieveECFR?gp=&SID=83cd09e1c0f5c6937cd9d7513160fc3f&pitd=20180719&n=pt45.1.46&r=PART&ty=HTML

Ember, S. (2015, March 19). Starbucks initiative on race relations draws attacks online. *The New York Times.* https://www.nytimes.com/2015/03/19/business/starbucks-race-together-shareholders-meeting.html

Emerson, R. M., Fretz, R. I., & Shaw, L. L. (2011). *Writing ethnographic fieldnotes* (2nd ed.). University of Chicago Press.

Encyclopaedia Britannica. (n.d.). Monopoly. In *Britannica.com.* Retrieved September 10, 2020 from https://www.britannica.com/sports/Monopoly-board-game

Fine, G. A., & De Soucey, M. (2005). Joking culture: Humor themes as social regulation in group life. *Humor, 18*(1), 1–22.

Fitch, K.L., & Sanders, R. E. (1994). Culture, communication, and preference for directness in expression of directives. *Communication Theory, 4*(3), 219–245.

Fitch, K. L. (2005). Preface to section V: Ethnography of communication. In K. L. Fitch & R. E. Sanders (Eds.), *Handbook of language and social interaction* (pp. 323–326). Lawrence Erlbaum Associates.

Flores, J. (2020, June 30). "A mask is not a symbol": Restaurants take a stand amid coronavirus pandemic. *USA Today.* https://www.usatoday.com/story/news/nation/2020/06/30/face-masks-required-restaurants-coronavirus/3283156001/

Fong, M. (1998). Chinese immigrants' perceptions of semantic dimensions of direct/indirect communication in intercultural compliment interactions with North Americans. *Howard Journal of Communications, 9,* 245–262.

Foss, S. K., Foss, K. A., & Trapp, R. (2002). *Contemporary perspectives on rhetoric* (3rd ed.). Waveland Press.

Garske, M., & Adan, M. (2020, May 21). *Customers, don't forget: Face masks required at dine-in restaurants, businesses in San Diego.* NBC 7 San Diego. https://www.nbcsandiego.com/news/local/customers-dont-forget-face-masks-required-at-dine-in-restaurants-businesses-in-san-diego/2329983/

Gioia, D. A., & Poole, P. P. (1984). Scripts in organizational behavior. *Academy of Management Review, 9*(3), 449–459.

Godoy, M., & Wood, D. (2020, May 30). *What do coronavirus racial disparities look like state by state?* NPR. https://www.npr.org/sections/health-shots/2020/05/30/865413079/what-do-coronavirus-racial-disparities-look-like-state-by-state

Goffman, E. (1959). *The presentation of self in everyday life.* Doubleday Anchor Books.

Goffman, E. (1963). *Behavior in public places: Notes on the sociological organization of gatherings.* Free Press of Glencoe.

Goldsmith, D. J., & Fitch, K. (1997). The normative context of advice as social support. *Human Communication Research, 23*(4), 454–476.

Gopnik, A. (2017, August 3). Norms and cliffs in Trump's America. *The New Yorker.* https://www.newyorker.com/news/daily-comment/norms-and-cliffs-in-trumps-america

Gumperz, J. J. (1992). Interviewing in intercultural situations. In P. Drew & J. Heritage (Eds.), *Talk at work: Interaction in institutional settings* (pp. 302–327). Cambridge University Press.

Hall, B. J. (1988–1989). Norms, action, and alignment: A discursive perspective. *Research on Language and Social Interaction, 22*, 23–44.

Hall, B. J. (1994). Understanding intercultural conflict through an analysis of kernal images and rhetorical visions. *International Journal of Conflict Management, 5*(1), 62–86.

Hall, B. J. (2017). Cultural communication norms. In Y. Y. Kim (Ed.), *The international encyclopedia of intercultural communication.* John Wiley & Sons.

Hall, B. J., Covarrubias, P., & Kirschbaum, K. A. (2018). *Among cultures: The challenge of communication.* Routledge.

Hart, T. (2015). Analyzing procedure to make sense of users' (inter)actions: A case study on applying the ethnography of communication for interaction design purposes. In T. Milburn (Ed.), *Communicating user experience: Applying local strategies research to digital media design* (pp. 27–56). Lexington Books.

Hart, T. (2016). Learning how to speak like a "native": Speech and culture in an online communication training program. *Journal of Business and Technical Communication, 30*(3), 285–321.

Hart, T. (2017a). Analysis of cognitive communication scripts. In J. P. Matthes, C. S. Davis, & R. F. Potter (Eds.), *The international encyclopedia of communication research methods.* John Wiley & Sons.

Hart, T. (2017b). Speech codes theory. In Y. Y. Kim (Ed.), *International encyclopedia of intercultural communication.* John Wiley & Sons.

Hart, T., & Achterman, P. (2017). Qualitative analysis software. In J. P. Matthes, C. S. Davis, & R. F. Potter (Eds.), *The international encyclopedia of communication research methods.* John Wiley & Sons.

Hart, T., & Milburn, T. (2019). Applying cultural discourse analysis to an online community: LinkedIn's cultural discourse of professionalism. In M. Scollo & T. Milburn (Eds.), *Engaging and transforming global communication through cultural discourse analysis* (pp. 21–34). Farleigh Dickinson University Press.

Henningsen, D. D. (2018). Deception in research. In M. Allen (Ed.), *The SAGE encyclopedia of communication research methods* (pp. 360–363). SAGE Publications.

Hepburn, A., & Bolden, G. B. (2017). *Transcribing for social research.* SAGE Publications.

Herring, S. C. (2007). A faceted classification scheme for computer-mediated discourse. *Language@Internet, 4,* Article 1. http://www.languageatinternet.org/articles/2007/761

Ho, E. Y. (2006). Behold the power of Qi: The importance of Qi in the discourse of acupuncture. *Research on Language and Social Interaction, 39*(4), 411–440.

Ho, E. Y., Lie, S., Luk, P., & Dutta, M. J. (2019). Speaking of health in Singapore using the Singlish term heaty. In M. Scollo & T. Milburn (Eds.), *Engaging and transforming global communication through cultural discourse analysis* (pp. 3–19). Farleigh Dickinson University Press.

Huspek, M. (1994). Oppositional codes and social class relations. *The British Journal of Sociology, 45*(1), 79–102.

Huspek, M., & Kendall, K. E. (1991). On withholding political voice: An analysis of the political vocabulary of a "nonpolitical" speech community. *The Quarterly Journal of Speech, 77*(1), 1–19.

Hymes, D. (1962). The ethnography of speaking. In T. Gladwin & W. C. Sturevant (Eds.), *Anthropology and human behavior* (pp. 13–53). Anthropological Society of Washington.

Hymes, D. (1964). Toward ethnographies of communication. *American Anthropologist, 66*(6), 1–34.

Hymes, D. (1972a). Models of the interaction of language and social life. In J. J. Gumperz & D. Hymes (Eds.), *Directions in sociolinguistics: The ethnography of communication* (pp. 35–71). Holt, Rinehart and Winston.

Hymes, D. (1972b). On communicative competence. In J. B. Pride & J. Holmes (Eds.), *Sociolinguistics: Selected readings* (pp. 269–293). Penguin.

Hymes, D. (1974). *Foundations in sociolinguistics: An ethnographic approach.* University of Pennsylvania Press.

Hymes, D. (1977). Qualitative/quantitative research methodologies in education: A linguistic perspective. *Anthropology & Education Quarterly, 8*(3), 165–176.

Ina, L. (1990, April 24). Wisconsin fights annual fishing war. *The Washington Post.* https://www.washingtonpost.com/archive/politics/1990/04/24/wisconsin-fights-annual-fishing-war/7bc29ba7-c340-42b6-94fb-3145b7df9315/

Ishihara, N. (2010). Compliments and responses to compliments: Learning communication in context. In A. Martínez-Flor & E. Usó-Juan (Eds.), *Speech act performance: Theoretical, empirical and methodological issues* (pp. 179–198). John Benjamins Publishing Company.

Johnson, D. (1988, April 24). Indian fishing dispute upsets north woods' quiet. *The New York Times*. https://www.nytimes.com/1988/04/24/us/indian-fishing-dispute-upsets-north-woods-quiet.html

Justice Information Sharing. (2013, September 19). *Title III of the Omnibus Crime Control and Safe Streets Act of 1968 (Wiretap Act)*. https://it.ojp.gov/PrivacyLiberty/authorities/statutes/1284

Katriel, T. (1985). Griping as a verbal ritual in some Israeli discourse. In M. Dascal (Ed.), *Dialogue: An interdisciplinary approach* (pp. 367–381). John Benjamins Publishing Company.

Katriel, T., & Philipsen, G. (1981). What we need is "communication": "Communication" as a cultural category in some American speech. *Communications Monographs, 48*, 301–317.

Keating, E. (2001). The ethnography of communication. In P. Atkinson, A. Coffey, S. Delamont, J. Lofland, & L. Lofland (Eds.), *Handbook of ethnography* (pp. 285–300). SAGE Publications.

Kivisto, P., & Pittman, D. (2013). Goffman's dramaturgical sociology: Personal sales and service in a commodified world. In P. Kivisto (Ed.), *Illuminating social life: Classical and contemporary theory revisited* (6th ed., pp. 297–318). SAGE Publications.

Kotani, M. (2002). Expressing gratitude and indebtedness: Japanese speakers' use of "I'm sorry" in English conversation. *Research on Language and Social Interaction, 35*(1), 39–72.

Kotani, M. (2016). Two codes for remedying problematic situations: Japanese and English speakers' views of explanations and apologies in the United States. *Journal of Intercultural Communication Research, 45*(2), 126–144.

Kuh, G. D. (2008). *High impact practices: What they are, who has access to them, and why they matter.* Association of American Colleges & Universities. https://secure.aacu.org/imis/ItemDetail?iProductCode=E-HIGHIMP&Category=

Kurylo, A. (Ed.) (2013). *Inter/cultural communication: Representation and construction of culture.* SAGE Publications.

Kvam, D. S. (2017). Supporting Mexican immigrants' resettlement in the United States: An ethnography of communication approach to building allies' communication competence. *Journal of Applied Communication Research, 45*(1), 1–20.

Lahman, M. K. E. (2018). *Ethics in social science research: Becoming culturally responsive.* SAGE Publications.

Lave, J., & Wenger, E. (1991). *Situated learning: Legitimate peripheral participation.* Cambridge University Press.

Lee, E. L., & Hall, B. J. (2009). Thou soo and aih auan: Communicating dissatisfaction in a Chinese Malaysian community. *Research on Language and Social Interaction, 42*(2), 116–134.

Leeds-Hurwitz, W. (2002). *Wedding as text: Communicating cultural identities through ritual.* Lawrence Erlbaum Associates.

Leeds-Hurwitz, W. (2005). Ethnography. In K. L. Fitch & R. E. Sanders (Eds.), *Handbook of language and social interaction* (pp. 327–353). Lawrence Erlbaum Associates.

Leighter, J. L., & Black, L. (2010). "I'm just raising the question": Terms for talk and practical metadiscursive argument in public meetings. *Western Journal of Communication, 74*(5), 547–569.

Leighter, J. L., & Castor, T. (2009). What are we going to "talk about" in this public meeting? An examination of talk about communication in the North Omaha Development Project. *International Journal of Public Participation, 3*(2). http://www.iap2.org/?403

Leighter, J. L., Rudnick, L., & Edmonds, T. J. (2013). How the ethnography of communication provides resources for design. *Journal of Applied Communication Research, 41*(2), 209–215.

Lindlof, T. R., & Taylor, B. C. (2011). *Qualitative communication research methods* (3rd ed.). SAGE Publications.

Lindlof, T. R., & Taylor, B. C. (2019). *Qualitative communication research methods* (4th ed.). SAGE Publications.

Littlejohn, S. W., Foss, K. A., & Oetzel, J. G. (Eds.). (2016). *Theories of human communication* (11th ed.). Waveland Press.

Logan, N. (2016). The Starbucks Race Together initiative: Analyzing a public relations campaign with critical race theory. *Public Relations Inquiry, 5*(1), 93–113.

McGregor, S. L. T. (2018). *Understanding and evaluating research: A critical guide*. SAGE Publications.

Merriam-Webster. (n.d.). Cognitive. In *Merriam-Webster.com dictionary*. Retrieved August 27, 2020 from https://www.merriam-webster.com/dictionary/cognitive

Milburn, T. (2004). Speech community: Reflections upon communication. *Communication Yearbook, 28*, 410–440.

Milburn, T. (2015a). *Communicating user experience: Applying local strategies research to digital media design*. Lexington Books.

Milburn, T. (2015b). Speech community. In K. Tracy, C. Ilie, & T. Sandel (Eds.), *International encyclopedia of language and social interaction*. John Wiley & Sons.

Miller, D. B., & Rudnick, L. (2012). *A framework document for evidence-based programme design on reintegration*. United Nations Institute for Disarmament Research (UNIDIR). https://unidir. org/publication/framework-document-evidence-based-programme-design-reintegration

Molina-Markham, E. (2012). Lives that preach: The cultural dimensions of telling one's "spiritual journey" among Quakers. *Narrative Inquiry, 22*(1), 3–23.

Molina-Markham, E. (2013). Being spoken through: Quaker "vocal ministry" and premises of personhood. *Journal of Communication and Religion, 36*(3), 127–148.

Molina-Markham, E. (2014). Finding the "sense of the meeting": Decision making through silence among Quakers. *Western Journal of Communication, 78*(2), 155–174.

Morrison, L. (2017, July 18). *The subtle power of uncomfortable silences*. BBC. https://www.bbc.com/worklife/article/20170718-the-subtle-power-of-uncomfortable-silences

Nemo, L. (2020, June 12). Why people of color are disproportionately hit by COVID-19. *Discover*. https://www.discovermagazine.com/health/why-people-of-color-are-disproportionately-hit-by-covid-19

Noy, C. (2017). Ethnography of communication. In J. P. Matthes, C. S. Davis, & R. F. Potter (Eds.), *The international encyclopedia of communication research methods*. John Wiley & Sons.

Philipsen, G. (1975). Speaking "like a man" in Teamsterville: Culture patterns of role enactment in an urban neighborhood. *The Quarterly Journal of Speech, 61*(1), 13–23.

Philipsen, G. (1986). Mayor Daley's council speech: A cultural analysis. *The Quarterly Journal of Speech, 72*, 247–260.

Philipsen, G. (1987). The prospect for cultural communication. In D. L. Kincaid (Ed.), *Communication theory: Eastern and Western perspectives* (pp. 245–254). Academic Press.

Philipsen, G. (1989–1990). Some thoughts on the perils of "critique" in the ethnographic study of communicative practices. *Research on Language and Social Interaction, 23*, 251–260.

Philipsen, G. (1990). An ethnographic approach to communication studies. In B. Dervin, L. Grossberg, B. O'Keefe, & E. Wartella (Eds.), *Rethinking communication: Paradigm exemplars* (Vol. 2, pp. 258–268). SAGE Publications.

Philipsen, G. (1992). *Speaking culturally: Explorations in social communication*. State University of New York Press.

Philipsen, G. (1997). A theory of speech codes. In G. Philipsen & T. L. Albrecht (Eds.), *Developing communication theories* (pp. 119–156). State University of New York Press.

Philipsen, G. (2000). Permission to speak the discourse of difference: A case study. *Research on Language and Social Interaction, 33*(2), 213–234.

Philipsen, G. (2003). Cultural communication. In W. B. Gudykunst & B. Mody (Eds.), *Handbook of international and intercultural communication* (2nd ed., pp. 51–67). SAGE Publications.

Philipsen, G. (2010a). Researching culture in contexts of social interaction: An ethnographic approach, a network of scholars, illustrative moves. In D. Carbaugh & P. M. Buzzanell (Eds.), *Distinctive qualities in communication research* (pp. 87–105). Routledge.

Philipsen, G. (2010b). Some thoughts on how to approach finding one's feet in unfamiliar cultural terrain. *Communication Monographs, 77*(2), 160–168.

Philipsen, G., & Coutu, L. M. (2005). The ethnography of speaking. In K. L. Fitch & R. E. Sanders (Eds.), *Handbook of language and social interaction* (pp. 355–379). Lawrence Erlbaum Associates.

Philipsen, G., Coutu, L. M., & Covarrubias, P. (2005). Speech codes theory: Restatement, revisions, and response to criticisms. In W. Gudykunst (Ed.), *Theorizing about intercultural communication* (pp. 55–68). SAGE Publications.

Pratt, S., & Wieder, D. L. (1993). The case of saying a few words and talking for another among the Osage people: "Public speaking" as an object of ethnography. *Research on Language and Social Interaction, 26*(4), 353–408.

Provis, C. (2012). *Individuals, groups, and business ethics.* Routledge.

Robles, J. S. (2019). Building up by tearing down. *Journal of Language and Social Psychology, 38*(1), 85–105.

Robles, J. S., & Kurylo, A. (2017). "Let's have the men clean up": Interpersonally communicated stereotypes as a resource for resisting gender-role prescribed activities. *Discourse Studies, 19*(6), 673–693.

Sabatini, P. (2020, June 26). Face masks "touchy subject" for local restaurants, but still required for employees under pandemic rules. *Pittsburgh Post-Gazette.* https://www.post-gazette.com/business/career-workplace/2020/06/26/face-masks-restaurants-COVID-19-Allegheny-County-Health-Department/stories/202006250144

Sandel, T. L. (2015). Rich points. In K. Tracy, C. Ilie, & T. Sandel (Eds.), *International encyclopedia of language and social interaction.* John Wiley & Sons.

Saville-Troike, M. (2003). *The ethnography of communication: An introduction* (3rd ed.). Blackwell Publishing.

Scollo, M., & Poutiainen, S. (2019). "Talking" and tapailla ("seeing someone"): Cultural terms and ways of communicating in the development of romantic relationships in the United States and Finland. In M. Scollo & T. Milburn (Eds.), *Engaging and transforming global communication through cultural discourse analysis* (pp. 129–155). Farleigh Dickinson University Press.

Scollon, R., & Wong Scollon, S. (2009). Breakthrough into action. *Text & Talk, 29*(3), 277–294.

Searle, J. R. (1969). *Speech acts: An essay in the philosophy of language.* Cambridge University Press.

Shoemaker, S. (1996, February). Scripts: Precursor of consumer expectations. *Cornell Hotel and Restaurant Administration Quarterly,* 42–53.

Silverman, D. (2005). *Doing qualitative research: A practical handbook.* SAGE Publications.

Silverman, D. (2013). *A very short, fairly interesting and reasonably cheap book about qualitative research* (2nd ed.). SAGE Publications.

Simmons, N. (2014). Speaking like a queen in *RuPaul's Drag Race*: Towards a speech code of American drag queens. *Sexuality & Culture, 18,* 630–648.

Sotirin, P. (2000). "All they do is bitch bitch bitch": Political and interactional features of women's officetalk. *Women and Language, 23*(2), 19–25.

Sotirova, N. (2018). A cry and an outcry: Oplakvane (complaining) as a term for communication practice. *Journal of International and Intercultural Communication, 11*(4), 304–323.

Spradley, J. P. (2016). *The ethnographic interview.* Waveland Press.

Sprain, L., & Boromisza-Habashi, D. (2012). Meetings: A cultural perspective. *Journal of Multicultural Discourses, 7*(2), 179–189.

Sprain, L., & Boromisza-Habashi, D. (2013). The ethnographer of communication at the table: Building cultural competence, designing strategic action. *Journal of Applied Communication Research, 41*(2), 181–187.

Sprain, L., & Gastil, J. (2013). What does it mean to deliberate? An interpretive account of jurors' expressed deliberative rules and premises. *Communication Quarterly, 61*(2), 151–171.

Starbucks. (2014, December 17). *A conversation with Starbucks partners about race in America.* https://stories.starbucks.com/stories/2014/schultz-begins-a-conversation-with-starbucks-partners-about-racial-issues/

Starbucks. (2015, March 16). *What "Race Together" means for Starbucks partners and customers.* https://stories.starbucks.com/stories/2015/what-race-together-means-for-starbucks-partners-and-customers/

Su, R., & Secon, H. (2020, May 16). *An interactive map reveals state-by-state rules for shopping at retail stores, eating at restaurants, and wearing masks in public.* Business Insider. https://www.businessinsider.com/map-us-states-reopening-retail-restaurants-masks-2020-5

Townsend, R. M. (2009). Town meeting as a communication event: Democracy's act sequence. *Research on Language and Social Interaction, 42*(1), 68–89.

Townsend, R. M. (2013). Engaging "others" in civic engagement through ethnography of communication. *Journal of Applied Communication Research, 41*(2), 202–208.

Tracy, S. J. (2013). *Qualitative research methods: Collecting evidence, crafting analysis, communicating impact.* Wiley-Blackwell.

Turner, V. (1980). Social dramas and stories about them. *Critical Inquiry, 7*(1), 141–168.

U.S. Department of Justice Civil Rights Division. (2015, March 4). *Investigation of the Ferguson Police Department.* https://www.justice.gov/sites/default/files/opa/press-releases/attachments/2015/03/04/ferguson_police_department_report.pdf

van Oudenhoven, J. P. (2013). Social scientific approach to culture: Representation and construction of culture. In A. Kurylo (Ed.), *Inter/cultural communication: Representation and construction of culture* (pp. 281–304). SAGE Publications.

van Over, B., Dori-Hacohen, G., & Winchatz, M. R. (2019). Policing the boundaries of the sayable: The public negotiation of profane, prohibited, and proscribed speech. In M. Scollo & T. Milburn (Eds.), *Engaging and transforming global communication through cultural discourse analysis* (pp. 195–216). Farleigh Dickinson University Press.

Wallis, C. (2020, June 12). Why racism, not race, is a risk factor for dying of COVID-19. *Scientific American.* https://www.scientificamerican.com/article/why-racism-not-race-is-a-risk-factor-for-dying-of-covid-191/

Ward, M., Sr. (2010). "I was saved at an early age": An ethnography of fundamentalist speech and cultural performance. *Journal of Communication and Religion, 33*(1), 108–144.

Weinstein, M. (2008). TAMS Analyzer. TAMS Analyzer for Macintosh OS X. http://tamsys.sourceforge.net/

Winchatz, M. R. (1999, February). *"Offering the du": Metapragmatic terms in German* [Paper presentation]. Western States Communication Association, Vancouver, BC, Canada.

Winchatz, M. R. (2001). Social meanings in German interactions: An ethnographic analysis of the second-person pronoun Sie. *Research on Language and Social Interaction, 34*(3), 337–369.

Winchatz, M. R. (2017). Jammern [whining] as a German way of speaking. In D. Carbaugh (Ed.), *The handbook of communication in cross-cultural perspective* (pp. 65–75). Routledge.

Witteborn, S. (2003). Communicative competence revisited: An emic approach to studying intercultural communicative competence. *Journal of Intercultural Communication Research, 32*(3), 187–203.

Witteborn, S., Milburn, T., & Ho, E. Y. (2013). The ethnography of communicaiton as applied methodology: Insights from three case studies. *Journal of Applied Communication Research, 41*(2), 188–194.

Wolcott, H. F. (1999). *Ethnography: A way of seeing.* AltaMira Press.

Zarroli, J. (2020, July 14). *The customer is always right. Except when they won't wear a mask.* NPR. https://www.npr.org/2020/07/14/889721147/the-customer-is-always-right-except-when-they-wont-wear-a-mask

Ziv, S. (2015, March 23). Starbucks ends phase one of Race Together initiative after grande fail. *Newsweek.* https://www.newsweek.com/starbucks-ends-phase-one-race-together-initiative-after-grande-fail-316043

Index